What to Say When They Say "I'm Jewish"

Sharing the Gospel with the Original Messengers

by
Dr. Fenton M. Ward

JOY PUBLISHING
PO BOX 827
SAN JUAN CAPISTRANO, CA 92675

Printed in the United States of America
10 9 8 7 6 5 4 3 2

International Standard Book Number 0-939513-86-2

Published by
Joy Publishing
P.O. Box 827
San Juan Capistrano CA 92675

Table of Contents

Part I: Developing the "Why"

Part II: Developing the "How"

FOREWORD

This might be one of the most important books you'll read this decade. If you'll apply yourself to this journey with Dr. Fenton Ward, he will guide you back through time, through culture, through your own fears, and land you safely on a shore of certainty.

You can **know** that it's right to bring the gospel of Jesus Christ to unbelievers, even when the world is shouting at you that if you really cared , you'd keep your religion to yourself. **And, you can know how to share that life-giving message effectively, even with those who seem unreachable.**

If you can witness to a Jewish person, you can witness to anyone. I know. As a Jew who believes in Jesus, I was once considered unreachable. In fact, over half the Jews for Jesus staff had a very negative first response to the gospel. Yet, here we are, many of us having come to faith through the witness of a Gentile Christian. A Christian like you. A Christian like Fenton Ward.

I have known Dr. Ward since the late 1970's, when he came to Tarzana Baptist Temple in Southern California. He was just beginning to work on his doctorate at Fuller Seminary in Pasadena. He attracted my attention for a number of reasons. First, he was the pastor of a Southern Baptist Church in an inner-city area, and he had an outreach to Jewish people. That made Fenton unique.

Then, I learned that Fenton was fairly fresh out of seminary when he took that pastorate. At age 37, he had left a ten year career in insurance and financial planning to attend seminary and become a minister. I admired him for his eagerness to learn at an age when many people seem ready to "coast" on what they already know. I admired his courage in leaving a secure income to follow God's call for his life.

We met over breakfast. Fenton was interested in Jews for Jesus because of his dissertation about Jewish involvement in churches. We were interested in him because he cared enough to tell our people about Jesus in a way they could understand. In fact, he chose the topic for his dissertation based on the fact that a core of Jewish people had begun attending his church and he wanted to figure out what to do with what he had.

Over the years, Fenton Ward's steadfast love for the Jewish people has touched me deeply. I think of the way he has attended Jews for Jesus Bible studies over the years—not to teach or officiate, though he is well qualified to do so. He came just to be with us, to sit and to serve in whatever capacity we asked. I greatly admire his servant heart.

As I read Fenton's manuscript, I was impressed by his ability to navigate through some sensitive waters. He has a rare sense of balance that enables him to maintain a considerate and caring attitude along with the courage it takes to proclaim the gospel without compromise. Too often I hear from Christians who want to take their cues on what it means to love from those who have not yet met the One who is the source of all love. Fenton's love is of the brave, faithful variety because it's a love that springs from his love of the Savior. Fenton Ward knows what it is to love the Jewish people the way Y'shua (Jesus) loved them . . . to risk being misunderstood and rejected by many for the sake of the remnant who will understand and accept Him. And you have to know, every day, there are Jewish people who are accepting Jesus. God is still working among His ancient chosen people.

Yes, Fenton Ward is a professional—a Baptist minister who's studied in the field and has been effective in evangelizing Jews. But he wants you to know that you don't have to be a professional minister to have a successful witness to Jewish people. As you prepare to read this book, I hope you'll be ready to learn how you can have a part in winning Jewish people to Christ.

As you read, you'll navigate through time and space to discover how Jewish people became predisposed to reject the gospel.

You'll learn about the differences between Judaism and Christianity.

You'll be equipped with specific tools to enable you to witness effectively.

You'll be released from the misconception that whether or not a person accepts Christ depends upon you and your ability.

You'll be ready for the joy of sharing the best news in the world with people who are dying to hear it.

This book isn't a lightweight "self-help" book. But, if your heart aches because you want to help others who are perishing without Christ, then this book will give you the courage and the confidence to do something about it.

Moishe Rosen, executive director, Jews for Jesus

Part I
Developing the "Why"

Chapter 1
IT'S NOT AS HARD AS IT SEEMS!

When you try to share the gospel with a Jewish friend, do you suffer a mental block? Take heart, there's a solution.

When you do share, are the two of you speaking different languages? Perhaps you make your point—quoting it right out of the Bible—and he isn't impressed! You share what you see as obvious, logical deductions. You build an air-tight case for Jesus—and does he say, "What must I do to be saved?" No. He says, "That's the silliest thing I have ever heard!"

It doesn't have to be that way. Any Christian who can explain why he is saved can tell someone else how to get saved—even if they are Jewish.

The phone rang as I sat in my office preparing for the morning worship. A very Jewish voice on the other end said, "You say in the Yellow Pages that you are a congregation of Jewish and Gentile believers. Is that true?"

"Yes, it is," I said.

"I didn't think such a thing existed. Are you a regular church...or...are you one of those groups that, well...that people would call a cult?"

I assured the man I would later meet as Sam that we were a regular church. I also assured him that a church could be very Jewish. He asked if he could see me before the morning service. Within ten minutes he was in my office, brought by a very common need. His story was not as unique as most would think.

Sam had grown up in New York in a religiously Jewish home. While researching a high school project on Christian art, he became curious about its inspiration. In a choice that seemed guided by God, he chose to read the New Testament, rather than a book about Christianity. Not daring to take this hated book home, he made frequent trips to the New York City library to re-read his forbidden find. As he read the scripture, he became convinced that Jesus was who he claimed to be—the Messiah of Israel and Savior of the world.

Sam tried to tell his family of his discovery, but they responded with disinterest at best and threats at worst. Soon his belief was his secret.

Later, Sam married and moved to Los Angeles. Only after leaving New York, did he share his conviction with his wife. Initially, she was horrified. Eventually, however, she came to the same view. They lived out their lives, raised their daughter to believe in Jesus, and kept this dark family secret to themselves.

They were an isolated trio. Rabbinic Judaism had no appeal because of their belief in Jesus. They visited churches, but never found one that overcame their learned fears. Not at home in either the church or synagogue, they worshiped alone through the years.

Surely in those years, Sam had crossed paths with other Christians. Apparently, no one ever told him that believing in his Jesus was what made them one. In his mind, he made no connection between a Jewish Jesus and current Christianity. To him, everyone who wasn't Jewish was Christian. He certainly didn't know that the early church was Jewish. Neither would he have guessed that the Body of Christ had continued to have Jewish members down through the ages.

Now Sam had a burden that he could not bear alone and so, again, he had chosen to gamble on visiting a church.

Four years earlier, doctors had diagnosed his wife as having cancer. He sold his business and became her around-the-clock nurse. Now she had died, his daughter was living in another city, and he was alone.

Sam stayed with us for worship that morning, but moved in a few weeks without leaving his forwarding address. Although he was glad to discover that he was not the only Jewish follower of Jesus, he had been isolated too long to join our church family easily.

Remembering Sam always brings several thoughts to mind, some comforting and some distressing. The fact that God saves human beings by the Holy Spirit's use of the scripture, not by human persuasiveness, comforts me. I'm glad God has the ultimate job of evangelism, aren't you? The Holy Spirit normally moves through us, however, along with circumstances as he did with Sam. Herein lies evangelism's limitation; it is the human element.

Sadly, we live in a day when Christians are almost universally reluctant to share the gospel. A study in a large evangelistic denomination found that only one out of a hundred members would ever lead someone to the Lord! Even in congregations that insist on an altar call, most ministers avoid one-to-one witnessing to those outside their church and its visitors. They suffer from what sales management labels "call reluctance."

Call reluctance is in every difficult form of sales; little wonder it also exists in evangelism. It hides in the process like minerals in the water of the Jordan River. Gradually, like the desert sun, rejection distills the joy out of sharing the good news. Soon what has been living water becomes a Dead Sea. If our joy is not replenished, our ability to witness will die from our fear of failure.

Many lack the faith to believe that God will use them as he promised. They expect others to lead people to Jesus, but not them. If you struggle with that, you are the victims of Satan's propaganda. His lie is that sharing your faith is a complicated process you will never master. It's not!

In its simplest and best form, the gospel is that people are redeemed by accepting what Jesus did for them as a gift. Memorize John 3:16—most likely you already know it—and explain it. You can see individuals saved with that simple witness. (If you would like some help in how to explain it, see the sample explanation in the Appendix. It's part of the commentary on key Scripture Verses.)

It is wise to know the cultural distinctions of those we try to reach. However, being an expert on the culture and unable to explain salvation leaves us ineffective. Understanding the truth of John 3:16 anchors the tight-rope of witnessing to those who are predisposed to avoid Jesus. Be encouraged! The basics are surprisingly simple.

The message we must convey is that one must depend on Jesus, what Jesus has done, and what Jesus will do for him, rather than depending on what he can do for God. However we say it, **dependence** is the human part of the bargain and is the critical element to convey.

I often wonder what Sam's life would have been like if someone had discussed Jesus with him years earlier. The story could have been different if he had found Christians who invited him into their lives before he chose to become a silent follower. He could have had the support of a church family in those difficult years as his wife lay dying.

I also wonder how many other Sams there are who are open to the gospel if someone would just discuss it. How many Jewish people would examine the gospel if we just brought up the subject? Surely, it is time for the community of born-again believers to stop assuming that Jews are not interested in Jesus and can't be reached.

A major goal of this book is to remove the expectancy of failure in sharing with Jewish people that Satan pumps into our minds. With that attitude, we are defeated before we start. Understanding how your friend thinks helps—and the coming chapters will help you do that. More importantly, you can do it because God has said so.

Chapter 2
HAS ANYONE SEEN JOHN, LATELY?

I met John in a much more casual way than Sam. His seat on the flight to Los Angeles was on the aisle; mine was at the window. John put his business papers in the empty seat between us as the flight attendant brought our meals. As we lowered our tray-tables, I asked, "Are you flying out, or going home?"

"Home," he replied.

"Been on a business trip?" I asked.

"Yes," he replied, and then he spent the next few minutes telling me about his sales territory. After a brief description of his work, he asked the inevitable question, "What kind of business are you in?"

My reply led to a discussion that occupied the balance of our flight. As we got our baggage and went our ways, John assured me that he would read the material I had promised to mail him. Moving to the bus stop for my commute home, I couldn't get John off my mind.

John had grown up in Northern California of pioneer stock. He had completed college without any disruptions. He now lived by values that would have made any church proud of him. Listening to his morals and values, most Christians would proudly proclaimed him a good Christian role model he was—but he wasn't. He was a good Jewish role model.

John's pioneer roots ran back to Sacramento, California, the oldest Jewish community of the West.

When others came to the American River to prospect in the gold rush, his forebears came to sell clothing and supplies.

In high school—and now in business—most of John's friends were not Jewish; he assumed they were Christian. His only knowledge of Christians, however, was that you couldn't be one if you were Jewish. Since he didn't attend synagogue, and was Jewish, he never suspected that the lack of Christian involvement in his Gentile friends should be any different. In his whole life I had been the first to tell him the gospel story, much less ask him to trust in a Jewish Jesus.

Like his other secular companions, John assumed that life came about through evolution. It was the only explanation he had ever heard. He felt there was probably "someone out there" but saw whatever that was as being like the Force of "Star Wars." He hoped there was an existence after death, but had no idea what it would be like.

Here was an attractive, moral young man, living by the standards of this "Christian nation." In spite of that, his only exposure to the Messiah was Christmas shopping and his friends' use of "Jesus Christ" as one of their expletives.

If John had been a derelict in downtown Los Angeles, someone in a mission would have told him about Jesus. To his detriment he was affluent and successful—two major factors contributing to his ignorance of the God who created him. Neither did he know that this same God loved him enough to die for him.

Again I wondered how many Johns were slipping through the cracks because of Christians assuming others are saved unless they signal they are not. How many, like John, have adopted the secular world-view their public school taught them, because no one ever challenged it? How many others have never heard of Jesus, because Christians didn't bother to share?

Few think about the needs of those who have a secular mind-set, be they Jew or Gentile. We forget that everyone comes to his world-view through a process that he regards as reasonable and logical. Very few are secularists out of a certainty developed by deep study; most are like John. Most have developed their views from a one-sided argument made in the absence of a Christian witness.

We fail to reach most Jews and non-Jews for the same reason. We assume they know the gospel and have already rejected it and we don't want to challenge those who have already made up their minds. We assume people are religious when they are not. In fact, the bulk of both—Jew and Gentile—are secular.

While it is certainly an advantage to understand the Jewish community, statistics show that it isn't mandatory. Jews for Jesus did a study of 8,000 Jewish believers, seeking to find the most productive source of persuasion. They found that the most effective witness was non-Jewish Christians.[1] The bulk of this practical witness was by people without any special Jewish evangelism skills. Even in cultural ignorance, John 3:16 is still an effective tool, if lovingly shared.

A major goal of this book is to combat our fear of failure. Remember? Being confident as communicators relieves fear—not to mention making us more effective.

The unseen danger we face is that as we talk, two half-conversations occur. Each person can hear something other than what is meant for each draws his definitions from different dictionaries! One borrows his dictionary from the church and the other borrows his

---

[1] Mitch Glaser and Beverly Jamison, *Demographic, Social and Spiritual Profiles of Jews Who Believe In Jesus*, (San Francisco: Jews for Jesus, privately published, 1983), p. 115.

from the synagogue. Neither realize Christianity and Rabbinic Judaism share common terms, but not common meanings. The upcoming chapters will introduce you to the Rabbinic dictionary of your friend so you can relate what you wish to share. They will give solutions to those communication problems—for you and for your Jewish friend.

Chapter 3
PLATO'S CAVE, REVISITED

In "The Allegory of the Cave," Plato tells a story of people who are chained so they can only look toward the rear of the cave. Unable to turn toward the mouth of the cave, they judge the shadows on the wall to be the reality. Thus, they form their world-view—their perception of reality—by assumption rather than by fact. Though it wasn't Plato's intent, this describes today's born-again Christians trying to share the gospel with Jewish friends. Even those who otherwise successfully share their faith often fail miserably when the friend is Jewish. Suddenly, most lack one—or both—of two critical resources: courage and understanding. Few know how their Jewish friend thinks—and few Jewish friends understand the intent of the messenger. As in Plato's allegory, neither recognizes the shadows on their different walls—as shadows.

Sociologists, anthropologists, and others call this understanding of reality, one's world-view. It is how we believe things are, whether they are or not. We form our world-view by what we believe in three broad areas. They are: (1) what we believe about God and the supernatural, (2) our opinions about man and human nature, and (3) what we believe about the world around us.

This is an important insight to grasp. If we just study Rabbinic **practices** and miss the attitudes that form them, we will never understand the Jewish world-view.

Society has challenged each generation of Christians with a world-view that was against the gospel; ours is no different. Gnosticism gave Christianity its first challenge. Secular Humanists are today's combatants.

If the Christian mind-set and the Humanist world-view are now in a struggle, with whom would Judaism side? Most Christians would answer, "With us!" They would be wrong.

A major misconception of Christians is that Rabbinic Judaism sees reality—except for who Jesus is—exactly as we do. The idea that we share a common Judeo-Christian heritage is a myth. (Our only common element is our ethical code.) If the Jewish people are "...branches that were broken off; that gentiles, the wild olive branches, might be grafted in...,"[2] then Rabbinic Judaism and secular Humanism are two twigs of the **same** broken branch.

Christianity, Judaism, and Humanism agree that human beings should be moral. Christianity, however, disagrees with both Judaism and Humanism about the origin of those moral standards. These stark distinctions get blurred by the emphasis on the standards, themselves.

There are Christians—who obviously have not read the Humanist Manifesto's definition of "Humanism"—who call themselves Christian Humanists. The terms, though, are mutually exclusive. Paul Kurtz, who edited the book, *The Humanist Alternative*, shows the irreconcilable difference between the two world-views when he writes:

> Humanism cannot in any fair sense of the word apply to one who still believes in God as the

---

[2] Romans 11:17

source and creator of the universe. Christian Humanism would be possible only for those who are willing to admit that they are atheistic Humanists. It surely does not apply to God-intoxicated believers.[3]

There are also cultural Christians. They follow the traditions and ethics of their church, but have the same temporal world-view as their society. They, to quote Paul, "...have the form of godliness but deny it's power."[4] Even born-again, dedicated Christians often accept the shadows as reality, merely because society says they are true. We accept the world's distorted views because we fail to seriously see Satan as the prince of this world.

Sadly, in the midst of this battle with the Humanists, we are no more prone to evangelize them than the Jewish people whom we think are our silent allies. We often feel intimidated by our assumptions about the education and affluence of both groups. Though we may show hostility toward Humanists as traitors for not seeing the universe through New Testament eyes, we patronize our Jewish friends. We excuse them from having to see truth as we see it. It is as if our beliefs were merely a Christian "esprit de corps," rather than being God's truth.

An added stifling impact on Jewish evangelism is our fear of being perceived as anti-Semitic. We are afraid to say Jews are as damned as Gentiles without Jesus.

Reversing our timidity is critical. Today, a shared philosophy of Humanism and Rabbinism speaks for the

---

[3] Paul Kurtz, ed., *The Humanist Alternative* (Buffalo, N.Y.: Promethus Books, 1975), p. 177.

[4] II Timothy 3:5

western world. A Judeo-Humanist world view molds our culture and the Christian voice is a minority report.

Any suspicion of misperception—about anything—dawns on few humans. Instead, we continue to assume everyone has our perspective. Truly, there are as many different assumptions as there are shadows on the walls of Plato's cave.

If we are to be effective, the first truth we must realize, as we turn toward the light, is that others do not see the world as we see it. Considering the number of scriptural references saying that, we should not be so surprised.

Chapter 4
THE WESTERN WORLD-VIEW AT THE END OF THE TWENTIETH CENTURY

Early in this century, the western world-view was still basically Christian. It was certainly monotheistic. Today, it is neither. While this change has increased secular opposition, it has also brought an expanded opportunity to share the gospel with the Jewish people—if Christians will act.

Early in this century, popular public lecturers spoke on the future as revealed in the Bible. They drew crowds from inside and outside the church. Today, prophecy is rarely discussed in church. Those outside think the whole idea is silly. This is because Western Civilization has shifted from a God centered view of our world to one centered on man. Today, even churches form more of their strategy from sociological studies than from a sense of God's guidance. We continue to judge reality by the shadows on the wall, not realizing that we no longer hold the lamp casting them.

This profane view of the world has also paved inroads for Eastern religions. Today, many perceive the supernatural as merely a heightened human ability, making it acceptable to liberal churches and synagogues.

College courses experiment with witchcraft and label it parapsychology. The polytheism of the East has been woven into Western thought by presenting God as merely the collective consciousness of humanity. Thus we come to find the predominate Western world-view of "God" is not Christian. Even our sense of divinity is man-centered, or secular, not centered on a Creator apart from his creation. Humanists, who make a place for the supernatural, see it as an extension of man's temperament and therefore not supernatural at all.

This reversal in focus from God to man has brought relief, rather than concern, to Jewish thinkers. This is because Rabbinic Judaism has centered more on man than on God for centuries. (A later chapter deals with this in more detail.)

The decrease in the popularity of prophecy—in church and out—says volumes about the change in the Western mind-set. It is a barometer because one's view about God is the basis of one's sense of reality.

The other major factors of one's sense of reality are his understanding of man and creation. If there is no God, or if God is merely the collective consciousness of humanity, then man is the height of an evolving self-generating universe. Or, if there is a Creator, but detached—as taught by Rabbinic Judaism—man is still the final authority on all questions.

How did Christians lose their role as molders of the national mind? How did we shift from a God-centered world-view to a man-centered one? It wasn't by any great global secret plot—at least not on the human level. Neither is it because those who see the world from a secular outlook are uniquely evil. Humanist convictions won because they were uncontested.

When the Humanists published their Manifesto in 1933, the churches ignored it. Thirty-four people signed it, most of whom were unknown outside of educational circles. One person stood out as its principal architect; he was John Dewey. In his lifetime, Dewey established the Humanist world-view as the foundation of today's educational ideology. This was a stroke of tactical genius! Through his influence on our educational system—and of those in other strategic areas—America gradually changed its perspective of reality. It has exchanged, bit by bit, its Christian world-view for that of the Humanist Manifesto.

The Humanist Manifesto declares that the universe is self-existent and not created. It considers the fulfillment of individual human potential as man's ultimate purpose. Today, most Rabbinic leadership would agree.

Humanism claims tolerance as its major virtue. In contrast, it pictures the church as bigoted, intolerant, and the major fountain of intellectual bondage. Rabbinic Judaism agrees.

Though the church has been guilty of this at times, the idea that those who accuse it are free from this sin is absurd. Today there are efforts to remove any trace of the Christian contribution to humanity's history. This certainly is something other than the "free flow of intellectual ideas."

Sadly, we have accepted this one-way tolerance at the cost of evangelism. It is a naive hope that our tolerance of non-Christian views will make those who hold them open to Christ's claims. The Bible tells us to be intolerant of non-Biblical views while being tolerant of those who hold them.

Well meaning Christians try to reconcile Christianity, Judaism, and Humanism. It's an impossible task. They say only "secular" Humanism is dangerous, yet the terms—secular and Humanism—mean the very same thing. The word "secular" means pertaining to the temporal (that is, concerned with worldly affairs) rather than the spiritual.[5] Secularism leaves no room for a creator God; the machine of nature is all that exists. In practice, Rabbinic Judaism leaves no place for God's intervention either.

Today, we in the Western world live in a society that assumes the Humanist view of reality is true. At the end of the last century, Western civilization assumed any non-Christian world-view was faulty. As we approach the end of this century, Western civilization assumes the Christian view of reality mistaken. Anyone who moves outside the church walls to share his faith must realize he ventures into a hostile world with an unpopular message. Thus, as the Jewish community becomes more open, the entire society stiffens against our declaration.

Again in our day, Christians must be lovingly militant. We must reject society's demand that we respect all views or be considered intolerant of all people. It tries to intimidate us by labeling us as ignorant bigots when we insist that contrary views can not be equally true! All men equally deserve our respect—even when they disagree with God. After all, we once did! On the other hand, only a fool would equally value all the ideas mankind has developed.

Biblical truths stand in conflict with what non-Christian views hold as reality—including those of Judaism. Trying to claim otherwise, to avoid controversy, papers over a fault line that will later rupture. If not, it will require continued compromise until we have nothing left to offer.

Obviously, people who hold non-Christian views of truth are not fools. They came to their view by what they felt was the best perception of truth. If they are

---

[5] William Morris, ed., *The American Heritage Dictionary of the English Language* (Boston: American Heritage Publishing Co., Inc., 1971), p. 1173.

honestly seeking the truth, however, and we are honestly speaking out of love, the respectful discussion of our differences will be rewarding.

Christianity disagrees with the basic Humanistic world-view adopted by society. It also disagrees with Judaism, which our Jewish friends have absorbed—whether they are religious or not. It disagrees with both because of what each believes about God, man, and man's relationship with God.

Recognizing—and saying—that Jewish people do not see the world as we do, does not make one anti-Semitic. Rather it makes one discerning about the shadows on the walls. Pretending they see what we see is not tolerant enlightenment; it is self-deception.

Chapter 5
HUMANISM IN THE JEWISH TRADITION

In the nineteenth century, the Jewish Enlightenment joined the European Renaissance in a commitment to their common Greek philosophical roots. The Jews of Europe left their ghettos and moved into society's main stream. This escape "into the light" came as German Jews discarded their Hebrew shell of traditions.

These ancient customs encased a world-view at odds with its own practices. Thus, Reform Judaism was born in an attempt to jettison peculiar Orthodox practices. They felt the **practices**, not the basic beliefs about God and man isolated them. Only customs, not perspective, separated them from their Renaissance neighbors outside their ghetto. The bid to join the outside modern ways and still "conserve" the Hebrew shell of traditions would later develop Conservative Judaism.

The horror of the nineteenth century Rabbis was the "modern ways" Reform Judaism brought. They were angry over the loss of the Hebrew shell, the traditional practices. The Biblical ideas of God and man, the basis of the traditions, had been replaced with a Greek world-view long before Jesus condemned the Pharisees for their hypocrisy.

Israel became Greek in her world-view in the inner-Biblical period. (These are the years of silence between the last prophet of the Old Testament and John the Baptist.) As Alexander the Great (334 B.C.) moved in conquest across his civilized world, the Greek glorification of humankind went with him. Greek influence continued to replace scriptural values in Israel well after the Maccabean revolt some 150 years later.

Greek philosophy eventually became so fixed in the Jewish mind-set that few in Israel recognized it as non-Biblical. The opposition to the Pharisees by John the Baptist and by Jesus was basically hostility toward their emphasis on the supremacy of man. Unknowingly, the Jewish culture had absorbed this central tenet of the Greek thought. Both of these prophets of Israel insisted she turn back to the Biblical claims for the authority of God.

In the days of Jesus, Jewish life was a variegated fabric of Greek and Biblical world-views. These concepts of reality fiercely competed for the minds of the Jewish people. Jews who embraced the Greek view of God, man, and nature, saw Jehovah as merely a local expression of Zeus. To them, Jerusalem was just another Greek city-state. In their desire to be Greek, they built a gymnasium next to the Temple and sponsored field and track events in the classic Olympic style of naked competition.

The Essenes were the other extreme. They rejected all Greek influence, both of outward custom and inward thought. They retreated to places like Qumran in disgust with Israel's spiritual adultery. There, they waited for Jehovah to vent his wrath on the decadent nation. Their attitudes were so much like those of John the Baptist that some have thought he was a member of their community.

The Sadducees and the Pharisees divided the center ground. The Sadducees, the more assimilated of the two, contained the priesthood and the Jewish aristocracy. They adopted Greek as their language—along with much of the Greek culture—but kept some Jewish traditions. The Pharisees, the direct ancestors of today's Rabbinic Judaism, held the "center right."

The Pharisees were the most powerful. They rejected Greek ways but accepted its central philosophical tenet—that man was creation's ultimate authority. The earliest record of Pharisees (which means to be separate) is found during the time of Jonathan Maccabee, in the century before Jesus. Current Judaism tries to link itself to Moses by claiming the early Pharisees as the rightful extension of these Biblical heros,[6] but the claim is invalid.

The Pharisees stressed the importance of practicing the Law, rather than what one believed to be true. While they zealously guarded Israel's orthopraxy (historically confirmed actions), Greek philosophy seeped into their orthodoxy (acceptably correct beliefs.)

This Greek breach through Israel's spiritual wall developed a Jewish elite enamored with Greek intellectualism and the Greek teaching system. Individual teachers (Rabbis) developed schools of scribes after the pattern of the Greek schools of philosophy.

Competing with the priests for power, the scribes separated the Law into two categories. They divided it into the sacred, which dealt with the eternal, and the secular, which dealt with the events of time. As

---

[6] "Moses received the Law on Mount Sinai and handed it down to Joshua, who handed it down to the Judges, who handed it down to the Prophets, who handed it down to the Men of the Great Synod..... Simeon the Just was one of the last members of the Great Synod.... Antigonos of Socho received the Torah from Simeon the Just..... Next came Jose ben Joezer and Jose ben Johanan.... Next came Johoshua ben Perakhjah and Nittai the Arbelite.... Next came Shemaiah and Abtalion.... Next came Hillel...." (quoted from Pirke Aboth, one of the most popular of Rabbinic documents.) Lewis Browne, ed., *The Wisdom of Israel*. (New York: Random House, 1945), pp. 126-127.

attorneys at law, they installed themselves as the experts in the non-sacred law—that is, the laws effecting day-to-day activities. Thus, they gradually isolated the influence of the Sadducean priesthood to the Temple. By doing so, they replaced them as the final authority on the Law in all matters of any practical purpose.

The Greek view, absorbed by the Sages of the Pharisees, was that man—in this case Jewish man—was the center of all things. Thus, in what would eventually become Rabbinic Judaism, the ultimate authority shifted to human intellect, separate from any divine control.

Seeing piety in external actions and reality on the basis of human logic, traditions became exalted over the scripture. These traditions—now known as the "Oral Law"—were considered equal to the five books of Moses and superior to the balance of scripture. No other Jewish group of Jesus' day recognized the Oral Law. To them it was merely an invention of the Pharisees to justify their authority.

In the latter half of the 400 years between Malachi and John, the Pharisees were the major voice in the local synagogues. They also held the majority power in the Sanhedrin, the religious court of the Jewish people.

Phariseeism, however, was not a unified ideology. There were as many schools as there were teachers. By Jesus' day, two had emerged as the most influential. One was rural and conservative while the other was urban and liberal. The rural conservative was Rabbi Shammai, more popular in the Galilean countryside, and the liberal urbanite was Rabbi Hillel of Jerusalem.

The Pharisees adopted the Greek exaltation of humanity. They limited it, however, to the descendants of Abraham who kept their version of the Levitical practices. Free from the hereditary limitations of the priesthood and open to anyone who would strive to live by their standards, they became the nation's most powerful religious group. And so they were when the

Baptizer came, calling Israel to repent of a self-righteous elevation of Abraham's descendants over Abraham's God.

Of the divergent Jewish religious groups, only two survived the fall of the temple in 70 A.D. These were the Christians and the Pharisees, the forerunners of today's Judaism. Rome destroyed the Essenes in the Jewish rebellions and the Sadducees, as priests, ceased to exist with the loss of the Temple. This reduced the field of combat for Jewish minds to its two final combatants, the early church (which was Jewish) and Rabbinical Judaism. Each now claimed to speak for God.

In human terms, Paul and others saved Christianity by exporting it into Gentile lands. This came just before the Jewish rebellion against Rome. Only one faction of Phariseeism survived. It represented one branch of the school of Hillel. It did so by being "exported" in the person of Rabbi Yohannan ben Zakkai.

Tradition has it that he had himself smuggled out of Jerusalem in a coffin in 70 A.D. while the city was under siege. Appearing before the Roman Legate upon his discovery, he pleaded for his life so he could develop an academy for the preservation of Jewish heritage. The town he asked them to spare for his school was Yevneh. Rome granted his request.

At Yevneh, Yohannan and his colleagues gathered all the available opinions on the Pharisees' Oral Law and organized these traditions into fixed legal categories. What they developed became the basis of Orthodox Judaism. Their emphasis was on Hebrew practice but their perception of truth was classic Greek.

With the decline of the Roman empire, the Rabbinic academies declined. As the lights went out in Yevneh, so too, the light went out in Europe as the Dark Ages began. The light also went out for Greek philosophy—at least in Europe.

As Islam developed into a world conqueror, the intellectual leadership of mankind shifted to the middle-East. Under the rule of the Sultans, Rabbinic scholars preserved the Greek classics. They also added to the world's intellectual material as Europe sank further and further into ignorance. During the Dark Ages, Judaism was the caretaker of the Greek philosophy that later became the source of the Renaissance.

The twelfth century brought both the apex of power in the Roman Catholic Church and the golden age of post-Biblical Jewish thought. Both fell victim to the same event, the Crusades.

European Jewry became the target of Crusaders on the way to "slay the infidel" in the Holy Land. This anti-Semitism pressed the Jews deeper into their ghetto life, from which they would not emerge until the nineteenth century. From its height in the twelfth century, the Jewish golden age stagnated into superstition. Nonetheless, Protagoras' view—that man is the measure of all things—survived at the center of Rabbinic Judaism. This Greek elevation of man, the hatred of their Christian oppressors, and the Hebrew shell of ritual formed the Jewish anchors of ethnic identity. Today's rabbinical Judaism rests on this unchanged tripod.

Meanwhile in the Gentile community, a recommitment to human freedom from Divine authority grew. It broke free in disgust with the Catholic Church's corruption and superstition. An attempt to throw off the authority of God now surfaced. It expressed itself in a drive to set up classic Greek reasoning as creation's highest truth. From this point Western man would seek his destiny within himself.

This resurgence of the old struggle between the world-views of Greek philosophy and the Bible only affected the Gentiles. Tradition had already locked the Jews into their own world. These traditions were—and are to this day—the Hebrew shell containing the same Greek view of man the Renaissance rediscovered.

In Europe the Renaissance of classical Greek values and its Humanism had been born and began to grow. Within the European Jewish Ghetto, it was already centuries old.

How does this impact today's society? Little wonder the leadership of liberal Christianity, Rabbinic Judaism, and secular Humanism agree in areas that range from national politics to ministry priorities. Their most visible commonality is the preference given to human concerns over worship concerns. Their common root is Greek philosophy, which makes man "the measure of all things."

The point of this review is not to campaign for any political view or ministry priority. It is to understand the Jewish mind-set as an important key to effective evangelism. (It is critical in reaching most non-Jews as well.) The shadows on the walls of our national cave make our society appear Judeo-Christian. In reality, it is classic Greek, or Judeo-Humanist, or more correctly, secular.

This is a major reason our evangelism fails when we reach beyond those of our own circle. We have unconsciously conditioned ourselves to share the Good News in a way that will only persuade those who already share our Christian attitudes. We only reach those who see the shadows shaped as we do. When we try to share in the same way with those of a secular mind-set, be they Jew or Gentile, they look at us as if we have been struck on the head! How to be effectively heard, rather than perceived as out of touch with reality, is our goal.

Chapter 6
PENETRATING THE MENTAL GHETTO

For all of the carnage of war, no picture will ever cause the shock of those first death camp photos of the Second World War. We saw corpses that moved, hollow-eyed, into the freedom provided by the liberators. They hesitated, fearful—not really knowing whether they were free or captured by a new exploiter.

The Jewish people with whom we try to share the gospel may be physically strong, but spiritually, they are equally disoriented. Worse, they fear that we may not have come to free them, but to eradicate them as a people.

We read in the fourth chapter of II Corinthians that the god of this age (Satan) has blinded the minds of unbelievers. Most read it as only applying to savages in hidden jungles, but that's not what it says. It says unbelievers—not uneducated. This includes moral, philanthropic Jews as much as any good, but lost, non-Jew.

Christians are not the only ones with misconceptions. Even after Jewish acquaintances become our friends, many will fear we are a potential danger to them! The Jewish community has been taught to view evangelism with the same dread and hostility as Hitler's death camps. In their eyes, its purpose is to erase the Jews as a people by their absorption.

Though the American Jewish community lives in a land with a church on every corner, they are cut off from the gospel. They are as separated from the Good News as the isolated tribesman at the head waters of the Amazon. Miles of anxiety and bitter blame separate them from our witness. Also, as primitive people resist missionary advances, so too, those of sophisticated non-Christian cultures resist our witness. Thus, most in the Jewish community are unwilling to expose themselves to Christian influence, including yours.

The two major Jewish fears are assimilation and anti-Semitism. They fear anti-Semitism as a violent threat and assimilation as a hidden danger. Generally, they see becoming a Christian as the ultimate assimilation. Other than the form, they see both as equally immoral and tragic. Both are perceived as the planned extermination of the Jewish people.

We must not, however, tailor our actions by their misconceptions. Though anti-Semitism is immoral and unacceptable, concern for the Jewish lost is not anti-Semitic! It is not sharing the gospel, but rather withholding it, that should be considered anti-Semitic.

Assimilation is entirely separate from one's beliefs about Jesus. It is "the process whereby a group, as a minority or immigrant group, gradually adopts the characteristics of another culture."[7] Being a Christian is not a matter of anthropology, it is a matter of conviction. In fact, most Jewish people who do not believe in Jesus are fully acculturated. They have adopted the majority culture, which is secular, not Christian.

Thus, **the first step** in sharing the gospel is to look for those who will allow you into their life. This is an

---

[7] William Morris, Editor, *The American Heritage Dictionary of the English Language*. (New York, Houghton Mifflin Company, 1971), p. 80.

important point! Remember, without some effort, you will never be a close friend to the Jewish people you know.

Generally, in the course of developing a friendship, a conversation will drift to religious questions. When your questions about God—or more likely, church—brings the response, "I'm Jewish," what have you found?

With rare exception, you have discovered a naturalist. As such, the idea of a god is a notion of the past. He, a thinking human being, has outgrown the need for these myths. Any truth not supported by the scientific realm is impossible. To the naturalist, nature is all there is, therefore environmental concerns almost reach the level of a religious commitment.

Man is the center of all things, the height of the evolutionary process. Man himself, not some external god, is the source of morality because he is essentially good. Evil will cease with improved education and the meeting of human needs.

On the other hand, he is a speck in the universe, a product of fate in a chaotic absurdity. Only random chance kept him from becoming a rock or a frog. As such, no god who might exist would notice him, much less intervene in his life.

For many the story ends there. Some are Humanists who don't even maintain a Jewish identity. Even those who maintain a strong Jewish identity still have a similar philosophy of life.

Though committed to a naturalist (or secular) world-view, the average Jewish American desires to have the best of both worlds. He maintains his Jewish identity, but wants to remain anonymous in the mainstream of American life. He selectively assimilates and faces a real tension over this inconsistency. In his self-identity, he must be an alien and a citizen at the same time. This divided loyalty often causes him feelings of confusion and ambiguity.

What then are the values a Jewish person would most likely have? He values education and the sophistication of urban life. He seeks to excel in a prestigious profession or develop his own business.

Religion is merely the expression of how people live ethically with their neighbors. Beyond that, the average Jewish person keeps those parts of his Jewishness that benefit him and exchanges the rest for whatever he pleases. In the end he maintains whatever level of Judaism he feels is necessary for his sense of Jewishness.

Jewish people are often ambivalent toward the non-Jewish world around them. On one hand, most are committed to a belief in the basic goodness of mankind. Thus, there is an expectancy—at least in theory—that the day will come when anti-Semitism ceases. On the other hand, the Jewish community believes that eventually, given the right circumstances, the Gentiles—whom they equate to Christians—will turn on it. One must defend the theory of man's basic goodness while ultimately expecting man's worst.

The Jewish person may be suspicious of non-Jews, and yet feel comfortable in the predominately Gentile secular society. Here Jew and non-Jew agree that religion should have no bearing on one's public life. Competing, Jewish people expect to perform above average. Generations of high self-esteem as God's chosen people helps—whether one believes in a god or not. There is also an ethnic excellence beyond the size of the Jewish population, and so he expects to compete successfully.

His visceral fear of persecution returns when he meets or hears of a zealous follower of Jesus. He remembers the long history of torment by the medieval church and expects those who seek to evangelize to have its attitude. He sees no difference between an attempt to persuade and an attempt to coerce. He divides his Gentile acquaintances into two groups. There are those who seek to convert others, and those who agree with him that such people are rude and dangerous! Few see themselves as Jewish because of religious beliefs; most have no strong view about God. Neither do they realize that born-again Christians are Christians because of conviction.

What then, makes one "a Jew?" One is Jewish by ancestry. It is **ethnic**, not **religious**, though the rabbis try to include religion as a necessary part of Jewishness. It is not religious because most Jews are Jewish without following Rabbinic Judaism. Except for the question of Jesus, what one believes about God is of no interest to the Jewish community. A Jewish person may be an Atheist or an Agnostic. He can be a practitioner of Zen-Buddhism, Scientology, or Mind-Science, and still be as Jewish as anyone else. His opinions about God are non-essentials.

The common view that Jewishness is both religious and ethnic is wrong. Being Jewish is ethnic, like being Irish. One who actively follows the prescribed practices of synagogue life is really Rabbinic.

Actually, one can not become Jewish by religious creed only. When a non-Jew converts to Judaism, he or she becomes Jewish because of their adoption as a child of Abraham and Sarah. Once they become Jewish—in this case by adoption—they are then eligible to participate in Rabbinic religious activities, if they desire.

As an adoptee, one receives the name of the adoptive family. Thus a man's name ends with "son of Abraham," and a woman's with "daughter of Sarah." The requirement to become adopted into the historic family shows that Jewishness is ethnic. The lack of any requirement of spiritual involvement or creed to maintain Jewishness shows that being Jewish isn't religious. Being "a Jew" is ethnic, not religious. One is Jewish by birth or adoption, not belief or philosophy.

Here is a critical insight! A major stumbling block for a Jewish person who is considering the claims of Jesus is his loyalty to his kinsmen. Jewish leadership has claimed for centuries that anyone who "converted" ceased to be Jewish. To reject one's Jewishness diminishes the Jewish community, just surely as the ovens of Dachau did. Conversion, then, is betrayal! No one treats this casually. Those who do not equip themselves to deal with this traitor factor, are on shifting sand. Do not assume that Jewish comrades will become Christian if they just understand that Jesus fulfilled the Messianic prophecies.

We can be more effective if we first communicate two truths. One is that true Christianity is a matter of conviction, regardless of one's genetic source. We must quit using terms like "Christian ways," and "Christian nations." There is nothing Christian, except individuals who trust the Christ. We must also make it clear that Jewishness is belonging to a sociological community—no matter what one's convictions are.

Religious dogma divides Rabbinic Judaism. Its three major branches are Orthodox, Conservative, and Reform. When non-Jews think of Jewish people, they predominantly picture the Orthodox.

Though cataloging the Jewish community as Orthodox, Conservative, or Reform is the most common way to try to understand their views, these labels are of little value. In fact, most Jewish people limit their synagogue involvement to attending on High Holidays. A better gauge of Jewishness is their sense of community and commitment to the Jewish heritage. Most live secular lives. Religious involvement for the majority—as is the case with Gentiles—is on a sentimental basis.

A better classification would be religious, cultural, and nationalist Jews. Most likely, you will not have friends who are religious Jews. These fit the stereotypical view of the Jewish community by non-Jews, but are a tiny minority. (The more serious the commitment and the more militant the form of Rabbinic Judaism, the less likely the person will have non-Jewish acquaintances.)

Primarily Israelis, nationalist Jews are concerned about Israel as a land, not the Jewish culture.

Cultural Jews form the largest cluster. They value Rabbinic Judaism as a necessary part of the Jewish heritage. Though they may not practice their Judaism, they will defend it because it is part of the "Jewish way of life." They may or may not "keep Kosher." They will vary in the degree that they observe traditions, but they will value them all. Even though they are not religious, they maintain a commitment to what they sense as "Jewish."

Few resist Christian claims as heresy against God. Rather, most oppose them as a threat to the Jewish people and their culture.

Chapter 7
WHY WE FAIL TO APPROACH JEWISH FRIENDS

Christians rarely share the gospel with Jewish friends because most don't take mankind's lostness seriously. Of those who do understand man's lostness, many erroneously see the Jewish people as automatically saved because they are "God's chosen people."

A small Christian minority worries about the Jewish people and realizes they are as "lost" as the bush-country pagan—or the Hollywood and Vine pagan. Those who involve themselves then face another reason few witness to their Jewish friends. It is that we are prone to **assume** our Jewish friend is an expert in the Old Testament, and are afraid he will ask us a question we can't answer! The average Jewish person, however, knows no more about the Old Testament than the average non-Jew knows about the New. Sadly, neither knows much about either.

We are also hesitant to share the gospel with Jewish people because we feel they are somehow our spiritual "elder brothers" and that it is impolite to correct our elders. Often, we have accepted the false view that Christianity grew out of Rabbinic Judaism.

Christianity is not Judaism's little sister. God did not change plans with the cross. Rather, the cross was a culmination of what God was teaching through the Levitical worship system and the prophets of the Old

Testament. Jesus was the fulfillment of that revelation from God, not a new insight. The right to claim to be an extension of Old Testament worship is with the church, not the synagogue. Chronologically, the church was 40 years old when what was to become rabbinical Judaism gathered its law codes and Pharisaical traditions out of a destroyed Jerusalem and began.

Another barrier is to forget that salvation comes individually. Thus, we must not neglect knowing a person on an individual basis in our quest to understand his cultural community.

Believers rarely seek the most critical information necessary for a successful witness and no one openly gives it. We have to discern it by listening to what interests our friend, rather than giving our witness mechanically.

Two factors have a huge bearing on how others react to our witness. Their openness to the Holy Spirit is the major factor and the other is their level of psychological need.

Sin and its bondage has warped us all. Remembering this will help us understand people's reactions. In our bondage, we learn that if we are to survive, we have to survive by the world's rules. "Rule No. 1" is that only the selfish survive. If you don't take care of yourself, nobody else will! "Rule No. 2" tells us to trust no one we can't control! This becomes the unconscious mind set of Jew and Gentile. However, as a persecuted minority, the Jewish people have learned a third rule; distrust outsiders.

If we exist in a cosmos that evolved out of some sort of primal soup, as the secular Humanist believes, then might makes right. If we live in a world left totally under man's supervision—which is a cardinal Rabbinic teaching—then the strongest will take what they want and the weak will die. If man is the only element in the equation, then it would be stupid not to be selfish and keep everything you get.

Though this analysis would horrify psychologists, they arrive at similar conclusions as to man's motivation. The purest expression of this is Maslow's Hierarchy of Needs, which is part of every beginning psychology class.

Maslow found man's most foundational motivation to be survival and security. Once a person is secure, he then seeks to meet his need to belong to some group. When he is comfortable with his sense of belonging, he begins to try to develop esteem within his group. In theory, when he attains that esteem will seek "self-actualization." Maslow also found that no one concerns himself with higher needs until he satisfies those that are elementary. Thus, we move up the path, one step at a time.

Remember what was stated earlier. Two factors have a great bearing on how people react to our witness: 1) their spiritual openness and 2) their level of psychological need.

How is this useful in sharing the gospel? Simply stated, each individual progresses in his spiritual growth and moves through set levels of felt needs. These are two halves of the same coin—which shouldn't surprise us! If we spot a person's place on the pathway of spiritual progress, we can avoid giving answers to questions he is not asking. Also, we need balance in our evangelism. We need to be bold, but not overbearing. Anyone can spot the extremes, but the correct balance is different for each person. Only the Holy Spirit can tell us how bold or how conciliatory to be.

Satan tries to push us off balance on the dove-side by saying that we must have an invitation to share our faith. The Great Commission says "Go!" not "Wait for an invitation." On the other hand, we can't bully people into the Kingdom.

We will offend occasionally, for the gospel does wound human pride, Jewish and Gentile. Any form of true evangelism incenses our naturalistic society. Society views religion as just one more human development along with literature, art, and music. It values all religions without requiring any foundation in truth. In reality, this tolerance is a view that all religions are equally useless. The thought is that since each religion is the product of the creative minds of each culture, it belongs to that culture. If each religion is the property of a specific society, no one should presume to persuade its members to abandon it.

If religions are only cultural, no one should evangelize anyone. Thus, many see persuasion as arrogant at best and immoral at worst. If, however, there is a God beyond nature who created nature, then he can do whatever he pleases with the tenets of each culture, directly or through his people.

Those who insist that we should not "force our views on someone else," violate their own demand. They try to persuade another that no one has the right to persuade another!

What then makes us too aggressive? This is a rare, but often cited, abuse. Jesus has very few zealots. When we are overzealous, it is often out of anxiety. Satan tries to convince us that God's love is conditional and that we must continually earn it. When he succeeds, we shift from sharing the Good News out of love to acting out of concern for our own reputation. If our reputation as one who is "on fire" is in danger, we may seek to see someone accept Jesus because of our needs. This shows, and is offensive to everyone.

Laziness is another danger. Though God is the major actor in the salvation drama, this does not excuse us from knowing our lines. When seeking to reach a member of any group, we need to do our homework, including discovering the group's uniqueness and the individual's current sense of need.

Why don't we share? Basically, we don't share because we lack faith. When we prepare and believe God will move in our friend's life—even against the odds—we relax. When we relax, we listen. When we listen—to our friend and the Holy Spirit—we discover that God can pull out of our preparation, just what we need to say.

Chapter 8
THE FORUM IS A DANGEROUS PLACE

Rome's public forum was in the center of the city and was controlled by an elite social class. A specific social class does not rule today's forum. Still, those who do control the public forum mold our morality and values. It is just a different elite.

When born-again Christians try to inject Biblical principles into society's values, they enter a hostile arena. That being the case, Christians must make every effort not to justify society's ban of our witness. We must be careful in what we say.

Many terms began in our language as slurs or vulgarities and with time became disjointed from their origins. Many people later use them without the intent of saying something insulting or off-color. The problem is that descendants of those against whom they were originally flung in hatred will be familiar with the original meaning.

We need to be alert to phrases in the general language that have offensive roots. Good and proper words often become hated tags because of who used them. For example, Jewish people should always be referred to, collectively, as "the Jewish people." We should refer to an individual as "a Jewish person." The terms "a Jew" or "that Jew" or "those Jews" may be grammatically correct, but they carry a load of emotional explosives from times past. Also, never use the term "Jewess" for a Jewish woman! There is almost a sense of expected rape in Jewish ears when they hear the term.

Another term to avoid is slang for making a shrewd trade. Many who don't mean to be cruel, talk about "Jewing someone down" when they get a bargain. The implication is that Jewish people care more for profit than for fairness. (How strange that we condemn this trait in others and take pride in it in ourselves.)

Ethnic humor is another well meaning but dangerous area. Every group jokes about itself and becomes the target of jokes by other groups. The soundest advice is to leave the ethnic jokes to ethnic comedians. Jokes that are funny when told "within the family" are seen as an attack when they come from the outside. No ethnic joke is funny enough to be worth the risk of alienating someone.

A phrase that should never have a place in the vocabulary of any Biblically literate person is the term, "Christ-killers." Shockingly, some still use it. It is a favorite anti-missionary complaint of the rabbis, but is a leftover from the anti-Semitism of another time and another place.

The born-again Christian should have no difficulty discarding this phrase or its theology. If Jesus died for all mankind, then all are equally responsible for his crucifixion.

Even if our explanation had advertising's most appealing imagery, we would still risk public ire when we share the gospel outside of church. The secular world views witnessing as an anti-social behavior when we try to persuade any outside of our own religious group.

The elite who dominate today's forum are self-elected on the basis of their own sense of intellectual superiority. They hold power through the attitude that only those who are intellectual—either actually so or perceived to be—have the right to persuade others of their opinions. The self-appointed elite do not judge truth on the argument's merits, but rather on the source's reputation. Thus, secular society intimidates those who seek to share their faith. It also intimidates those who would like to hear the gospel, but who fear the results of getting caught listening.

Current society will never give us a fair opportunity to share. The sooner the believer becomes realistic about his world, the sooner he will be free of the false hope that others will admire him for his obedience to the Great Commission.

Jesus repeatedly said that the world would not accept us, yet too many Christians continue to crave acceptance. They hope that if they allow society to dictate the conditions for witnessing, that it will approve.

Secular society, with the approval of Rabbinic leaders, tries to block our witness by disqualification. It asserts that any Christian who would be so ill-mannered as to try to "proselyte" a non-Christian must be ill-bred and anti-social. With such a judgment, they disqualify others from deserving to speak.

To be heard by a Jewish mind, we must explode this view that we are—by definition—undeserving to be heard. To do so, we have to be sure of our facts and state them with confidence. Both halves are critical. If we cut corners and pronounce something as truth that isn't, Satan will expose our exaggeration and destroy our integrity. If we are not assertive when faced by an intellectual bluff, or a sincere error, we will lose our credibility.

The process of persuasion follows the dynamics of debate. One does not begin by arguing for his final point, but by showing why it is not unreasonable for him to hold it. Only after your view is accepted as a potential, will arguments for its validity be heard. The goal at this stage is to get the Jewish person to think for himself.

The most important thing to remember when we enter society's forum to "lift up Jesus" is not to allow the intellectual world of the naturalist to intimidate **us**. We must be assertive with the truth. Here is a very important key to human nature! A speaker's self-confidence is often a more persuasive factor than his logic!

All decisions go through a series of filters, each of which is a major hurdle. These are easier to see if we look backward through the process of how one comes to trust Jesus.

To trust our God, our friend must trust the direct witness of the Holy Spirit. To do that, most will need our encouragement. To trust our witness, he must first trust us. To trust us, he has to be sure we are competent. If we don't reflect competence, why should he trust what we say? The purest truth, given in a way that does not inspire confidence, will never be heard, much less considered.

We can also smooth out the process by anticipating and answering our friend's objections to what we are saying before he makes them. If we answer objections before people raise them, people don't have to defend them. Not having to defend them, they can give them up without losing face.

Remember, too, people do not start with their honest objections. They will give the objection they think will stop you. They hope you will then go away and not force them into a decision which they fear may be a mistake. If you doubt this, remember what you said to the salesman who assured you "this is the car for you!" when you weren't so sure it was.

Last, we need to share our witness with friends a little at a time, testing their response as we go. If we remain active in the forum, we don't have to move our friend from being a naturalist to an apostle in one step!

Chapter 9
THE RABBIS AND REVELATION

The purpose of this and the next chapter is not to make you an expert on Rabbinic thought, but to clear away any misperceptions about what Rabbinic Judaism teaches. Christians are shocked when they discover that Rabbinical leadership disagrees with them about much more than who Jesus was!

What though does the rank and file of the Jewish community believe? Again, our assumptions are wrong. The rank and file neither believe what most Christians believe, nor the bulk of what Rabbinic Judaism teaches. Most have the same secular beliefs as their non-Jewish friends. Only in their case, it has been colored by Rabbinic views absorbed through the Jewish culture.

Most assume that if there is a God, doing the best you can is all He has any right to expect. The rest figure that it is an irrelevant question because, "when you're dead, you're dead."

For most of America's irreligious—Jew and Gentile—the question of religion is a question of ethics, not worship. For them, all religions are equally good, because all have (in their mind) the same moral code, that is, "be a good person." Questions about God, sin, heaven, hell, and so on, are inventions of the various clergy.

Most of the irreligious form their views from a foggy mix of input they unconsciously absorb. Most people believe there is a Creator God because it is the best explanation of the creation around them. Beyond that, their view of that God is molded by the degree of religious instruction—direct or second-hand—that they absorb. Thus, Rabbinic teaching impacts almost every Jewish life. However, for the irreligious majority, it has been diluted to a vague shadow.

From the time Christianity replaced paganism as Rome's official religion, the Bible has been the ultimate authority on God in Western civilization. In the past, the debate was over what it meant. Now, most arguments are over whether it is God's word or man's literature. Thus, past evangelism training equipped its students to answer the objections of people who believed the Bible but who didn't want to obey it. Facing a people, though, who only see the Bible's greatness in its literary contribution, our evangelism falters.

Foundational to all other theological questions is the question of revelation. Where do we get what we believe about God? Does God reveal it to us; or does man discover it?

On this question hinges the major contention between Rabbinic Judaism and classic Christianity. There is little argument over what any specific text says; the disagreement comes over what it means. Nothing effects this question of meaning more than one's view of the source of the Bible.

Most Christians come to the Bible seeking what God has disclosed. Most Rabbinic thinking is based on what human beings have discovered about God. Disagreeing at this initial point, classic Christianity and Rabbinic Judaism move farther and farther apart with each issue.

The Talmudic sage is Judaism's parallel to the Christian theologian. The sage, however, searches the Talmud to enhance Jewish culture. His insights add to the refinement of the Jewish code of conduct. It is not primarily a search for God, but for rules of conduct.

Like other law codes, Rabbinic law is a growing body of material. Built over the centuries, it is somewhat like an onion. It has layers of development we must peel away to investigate and understand the whole.

The "outside skin" of this code is the Halakah and the Aggada. Halakah, meaning "to walk," is the Hebrew term for the laws. An observant Jew tries to follow these "in his daily walk." The Aggada is the folklore of the Jewish people. The authority for the religious Jew is the current Halakah. It prescribes what to do in any set circumstance.[8]

The basis of the Halakah's authority is the Talmud. This is the layer just beneath the skin. The Talmud is a collection of Rabbinic opinions from around 500 A.D. A major part of these come from an older collection known as the Gemara. The Talmud consists of comments by various rabbis on older Rabbinic views—agreeing and disagreeing—plus decisions on the interpretation of scripture passages. Fundamentally, it is a collection of everything that anyone of any importance before 500 A.D. ever said about anything. It is organized by subject rather than by scripture text.

The Gemara, a major source of the Talmud, is an extension of an earlier collection of laws and opinions, known as the Mishnah.

Rabbi Judah Ha-Hasi (the Patriarch) assembled and edited the Mishnah around 200 A.D. It then became the official legal code in his day. He compiled it from oral traditions and named it after the Hebrew word meaning "a study."[9] Together, this body of traditions make up what is known as the Oral Law.

---

[8] Morris Alder, *The World of the Talmud* (New York: Schocken, 1963), p. 60.

[9] Ibid., p. 35.

The base for the Halakah—today's binding law—rests on the five books of Moses, plus—to the shock of most Christians—the oral traditions. While the thought of traditions having superiority to parts of the Old Testament is outlandish to most Christians, it is a basic assumption in Jewish thought.

Those who believe inspiration is merely human discovery naturally expect to supplement that discovery with improved insights. Each generation has its own wise men with contributions to make. Since their contributions are of value, they must be inspired, too. If they are inspired, like Samuel or Isaiah, their views are proper additions to the Oral Law. Gradually, the definition of inspiration drifted from the direct speech of God to Israel (as recorded in Exodus 19) to being equated with gifted human intellectual discovery.

This Rabbinic understanding of inspiration has many ramifications. First, study reveals that the Oral Law varies on common points. Sages solved this by the notion that some traditions have more authority than others. It is then an easy step to believe sections of the Old Testament also vary in authority.

If the authority of the commands vary, people are free to judge which of God's "commands" are binding and which are optional. If inspiration is a matter of human genius, another genius can surpass older inspiration and alter it.

Rabbinic leadership overcomes the dilemma of obedience to ancient practices by seeing the Word of God as allegorical rather than literal. Allegory is a literary device that hides a deeper message in a story with parallel events. For example, Gulliver's Travels is a political allegory, written as a fairy tale. This is fine for literature, but when applied to scripture, it changes the message. It destroys the literal record by suggesting there is a deeper significance. Worse, it allows the reader to claim whatever deeper meanings he likes.

Rabbinic sages feel allegory is a good and acceptable approach to reconciling the Bible with modern needs. A well known Jewish expert on this subject, Robert Gordis writes:

> Since the Bible is the Word of God, every apparently unimportant word and insignificant incident must have a **deeper** meaning. This view that it is to be approached allegorically became the basis of the weight of material that makes up the Talmud. If the scripture's meaning is to be found through allegory, then the **interpretation** becomes more important than the literal text.[10]

Early Jewish scholars gave their attention to the exact words and letters that made up the Old Testament. The Masorets, for example, existed to guarantee the exact copying of scripture. Now, search for the evolving significance has replaced the stress on the specific statement of the language. Little wonder that Jewish people are no more prone to accept the Bible as the final authority than secular Gentiles. Both the world and the rabbis suggest that the Bible is ONLY a collection of human wisdom.

---

[10] Robert Gordis, *Poets, Prophets, and Sages* (Bloomington, Indiana: Indiana University Press, 1971), p. 6. (Emphasis is mine.)

Chapter 10
WHAT ABOUT SIN, ATONEMENT, AND THE AGE TO COME?

Sin is a common term in the Christian and Rabbinic vocabulary. Both agree that sin is a transgression.

For Christians, sin is—first and foremost—against God, even in those cases where the direct injury is to fellowman. In Judaism all sins are against humanity. For example, it sees the sinner himself as the injured party when the sin is against God. To fail to keep God's commandments is to live below one's potential, thus violating oneself. "Sin is rebellion against God, **but more seriously yet,** Judaism considers it the debasement of man's proper nature."[11]

The Rabbinic sage explains human moral failure by saying there are conflicting drives within us. One drive is to do good. It is called the "yetzer ha-tov," the good inclination. The other is the "yetzer ha-ra," the bad inclination. Sin results when man allows his yetzer ha-ra to overpower his yetzer ha-tov. In the Rabbinic system, we need both, even though the evil inclination causes us to commit unacceptable acts. Man gets his ambition from it, and without it, he would not engage in competitive commerce or develop a profession. It is the source of all forms of appetite as well. It is both the

---

[11] Arthur Hertzburg, *Judaism* (New York: George Braziller, 1961), p. 195. (Emphasis is mine.)

source of sexual misconduct and the drive to marry and propagate the race.

What though, is one to do when his "yetzer ha-ra"—his evil inclination—gets the best of him and he sins? Both Christianity and Rabbinism say, "repent." Here again, what seems to be common ground is not!

For the Christian, the "turning" of repentance means to **turn away** from sin and to **turn to** God for forgiveness. The Rabbinic meaning of repent is also to turn away from sin but it is to **turn again** to man's true sin-free nature.[12] One's repentance—returning to his true self—erases the sin produced when he ceased to "be himself." Thus, Rabbinic thought needs no atonement or mediator between God and man.

Obviously, stressing that Jesus died for our sins is ineffective with a person who thinks that quitting whatever he did wrong has already erased them!

Christians fail to grasp the reason for the Jewish rejection of Jesus as the Messiah. Most reject him because they have grown up being told to reject him. They don't know why, they just know their community expects it. Judaism, however, rejects Jesus—not because of historic study—but because they don't believe mankind needs a mediator.

In Rabbinic thought, man does not stand before God, either as acceptable or unacceptable because of what he is. Rather, he successfully stands before God by being good enough.

Rabbinic Judaism rejects any need for a vicarious atonement for sin. Man does not have this need. Being made in the image of God, he was never separated from God. Regardless of his conduct, he has the potential of correcting his sins by returning to the proper course of action. Since we can make any needed correction ourselves, we need no mediator.

---

[12] Hertzberg, *Judaism*, p. 195.

In turn, if man can approach God on his own merit, God coming to man's aid as a mediator is unnecessary. Worse than that, it would be an interference with human progress and man's job as perfecter of creation.

Judaism sees man as his own mediator, based on the opinion that humanity is not cut off from God. It sees God's creation of man in his image as an unbreakable link. The practical use of knowing this in evangelism is to realize that we must show our Jewish friend that he is lost before he will be willing to be found. (Later chapters will show how to do that.)

Jewish sages reject any limitation, spiritual or otherwise, inherited from Adam and his disobedience. They reject this as unjust of God and therefore impossible. On the other hand, Israel and the Jewish people enjoy favor with God because of Abraham and other religious forebears through the ages. This is having it both ways. They reject original sin through Adam, but accept "zekut Aboth," which is benefiting from the merits the Patriarchs. Both are central positions. In each case, the ancestor's obedience or disobedience of God affects their life. Yet, the rabbis accept one as a factor and reject the other.

What then about the age to come? Both Christian theologians and Rabbinic sages base their view of the age to come on the same scriptures dealing with the Messiah's rule and kingdom. They disagree, however, about what these terms mean.

The Christian speaks of a Messiah who is a person and who relates to him. The rabbi disagrees; few even see the Messiah as a person. Most of Rabbinic Judaism has abandoned the idea of an individual Messiah. For them, Messianic rule will be a period of significant Jewish world influence. Those who expect an individual anticipate a government official, rather than a personal savior.

At best, Rabbinic leaders gloss over the Messianic promises in which Christians see Jesus. They read Messianic "prooftexts" as referring to the nation, Israel. They claim Christians take these scriptures out of context or misapply them—or that they are pictures not to be taken literally. These views are the product of the less traditional side of Judaism, but they have filtered into the beliefs of the more orthodox as well.

With rare exception, the Jewish people themselves claim to be waiting for the Messiah, but they have no concept about who he will be or when he will come. They just know that a difference between Rabbinic Judaism and Christianity is over whether the Messiah has come or not.

The bulk of Judaism claims the prophets merely expressed Messianic ideals for Israel in the literary form of an ideal person. They also believe that the prophets used the form of a kingdom, as well as a person, to express these ideals. Continuing this evolution of the Messianic Kingdom, the Rabbinic sages progressed from a King to a perfected democracy.[13]

In the latter half of the nineteenth century, the early leaders of the Jewish Reform movement saw mankind moving toward Utopia. Like liberal Christians, they expected man's growing enlightenment to solve all problems. They believed the Messianic age was beginning to dawn in their day. Mankind was striding rapidly toward universal education, social progress, and material abundance. However, the rise of Nazism in the most enlightened nation of the earth crushed this utopian dream.

The Zionists saw their movement as the Messianic hope. They embraced the Messianic ideals in their hope of the restoration of Israel. Rejecting a belief in a

---

[13] Jocz, *The Jewish People and Jesus Christ*, p. 296.

personal Messiah, they would bring in the kingdom as a Jewish nation.

Though some describe the Messiah in terms that show a competence only held by God, they refuse to add redeemer to his job description. For example, Joseph Klausner, a Rabbinic scholar on this subject, is still inconsistent. Along with others, he insists that political and spiritual redemption do not require a personal messiah. This reasoning comes from the fact that only God can save and therefore, to be a spiritual redeemer, the Messiah would have to be God! Yet, Klausner describes the Jewish belief in the Messiah as:

> ...a strong redeemer, (who) by his power and his spirit, will bring **complete redemption**, political and spiritual, to the people of Israel, and along with this, earthly bliss and moral perfection to the entire human race."[14]

Christians conclude that if only God can save, the completely redeeming Messiah must be God. This is not acceptable to Rabbinic logic.

Current leaders downgrade the subject of the Messiah. This is because answers to the questions this subject raises are too close to what Jesus' followers have claimed for centuries. Thus, many Rabbinic answers are reactions to Christian beliefs, rather than responses to an unprejudiced study.

Furthermore, the idea that today's Rabbinic evolution away from a "slaughterhouse religion" might be temporary, is unthinkable. Returning to a religion based on blood is far too repugnant for today's cosmopolitan Jewish mainstream. Louis Jacobs reflects this when he says: "We simply do not see the matter at

---

[14] Joseph Klausner, *The Messianic Idea In Israel* (New York: The Macmillan Company, 1955), p. 9. (Emphasis is mine.)

all in this way and do not believe it will ever happen in this way."[15]

In summary, Rabbinic Judaism expects the Messiah to be a great political leader. He will arrive and bring a one-world "Utopia" with Jerusalem as its capital. It understands the Messianic age to be the product of mankind's evolution toward perfection, exemplified in Israel.

What then about life after death? Christianity and Rabbinic Judaism disagree about its specifics and its importance. To Christians it is central; to Judaism it is incidental.

Rabbinic Judaism may speculate on questions of man's future after death, but it is merely speculation in a religion of ethics. It sees no break between God and man. If paradise exists, it assumes everyone will be there.

An example of the low priority in Rabbinic thinking of life after death is a comment beginning the chapter "The Life to Come: Resurrection and Judgment" in Montefiore and Loewe's *Rabbinic Anthology*. Their comment is as follows:

> I propose now to close this anthology with some quotations concerning the Rabbinic views about the life beyond the grave. These extracts will not be very numerous, because while the Rabbis knew no more about the future than we, they thought about it in terms and conceptions most of which have become obsolete and remote for

---

[15] Jacobs, *A Jewish Theology*, pp. 299, 300.

us today, and so their ideas are of small interest or profit.[16]

Rabbinic beliefs about the world to come grew in the period between the fall of the Temple and 200 A.D. Today, most view the subject as antiquated and embarrassing.

Now, Rabbinic scholars believe the earlier writing on the resurrection was a mix of Greek and Persian ideas. They see it developing from the Greek belief in the pre-existent soul and the Persian hope of resurrection. They think these were fused with the Hebrew desire for a Messiah to form the concepts of the Hereafter.[17]

Those rabbis who expect a life after death, expect it for all mankind with some exceptions. Here too, there are inconsistencies. They expect God to regather all men into Eden. Since man never fell, all keep the capacity to be divine. Yet the Jewish sense of justice requires that God reject some—such as the S.S. leaders of Nazi Germany.

The rank and file of the Jewish community give little thought to the question. Most assume they are going to "heaven" because of sheer human hope. The others believe that when you are dead, you are dead, and that's the end of it.

---

[16] Montefiore and Loewe, eds., *A Rabbinic Anthology,* p. 580.

[17] Jacobs, *A Jewish Theology,* p. 306.

PART II
DEVELOPING THE "HOW"

Chapter 11
SIGNPOSTS ALONG THE WAY

With this chapter we begin the specific, step by step, decision process which those who come to God follow. Though we deal with the process as steps, we must avoid thinking of this as mechanical. These serve as check-points. Few realize they progress though these steps, but each person does, consciously or unconsciously.

God draws each person in a unique way, but there is a general pattern. This pattern is a major subject in James Engel's and Wilbert Norton's book, *What's Gone Wrong with the Harvest*. They place prospects on a scale that runs from a minus eight to a minus one. (Minus eight is a person who is aware of a Supreme Being but who has no effective knowledge of God. Minus one is a person at the point of repentance and faith in Jesus. They also have a plus scale for Christian growth.[18])

Ralph Neighbor, Jr. uses the same concept in his "TOUCH" Evangelism, (Transforming Others Under Christ's Hand.) He illustrates the same truth with a pyramid whose broad base is made up of those unaware of God.

Engel, Norton, Neighbor, and others have discovered the same process. They all suggest that to

---

[18] James F. Engel and H. Wilbert Norton, *What's Gone Wrong with the Harvest?*, (Grand Rapids, Zondervan, 1975), p. 45.

witness, effectively, we must discern the spiritual position of our friend. Thus, if we are aware of a mountain trail that our friend is climbing, we can move along it until we find where our friend has sat down to rest and think. Then we can deal with his questions until he is ready to get up and climb again. Later, when he gets his path blocked by a new doubt, we need to cut away the brush and clear the boulders with the right answers.

Most current evangelism programs start mid-trail because they are designed to reach those already within a church's influence. Generally, those programs presume a respect for, and some knowledge of, the Bible.

Such programs are often ineffective with Jewish people because most Jewish people do not regard the Bible as the word of God. Further, they feel that only rabbis can interpret Scripture and therefore don't expect to understand it themselves.

All people move toward God in the same fashion; Jewish people just have some additional stops along the way with more possibilities of becoming side-tracked.

In the following chapters we will illustrate this process by eavesdropping on the evangelistic conversations of an imaginary friend. We will call him "Charlie," and listen as he shares with those in his life.

It would be nice if everyone understood and trusted us, and so allowed us to share the gospel openly. It would also be nice if they followed this script by the light God provides. Most Jewish people, as well as those of other non-Christian people-groups, will not. It is more likely that progress will be halting with many stops and starts.

As mentioned before, most Jewish people will not expose themselves to Christian relationships. Many who are willing to see us socially, will hold us at the acquaintance level. This protects them from an open discussion of God. The fact that we know someone does not mean they are our friend. The point is, pushing beyond what an acquaintance is willing to discuss is counterproductive. (This is not a recommended strategy for cross-cultural missionaries, but for those of us who are attempting to reach friends. Confrontation is an important part of the process but should be left to those called to do it.)

How then, will we recognize when they are ready to hear us? To recognize our time of opportunity, we must listen! We must listen to the Holy Spirit, and listen to what our friend is saying—behind his actual words.

He may tell you that he doesn't want to talk about "religion." If so, drop the subject and wait for another day to bring it back up. To continue to press, or to drop the subject forever, is wrong. Your friend may also be willing to tell you his opinions on religion, but not willing to listen to yours. A classic case of this occurred to me. I was buying a book in a little Jewish book store when the owner asked about my interest in Jewish beliefs—since it was obvious that I wasn't Jewish. As the conversation began to develop, he took it upon himself to tell me that we both "worship the same God, etc." When I disagreed with some of his instruction on Christianity, he cut me off with "I don't want to talk about religion." The truth was that he didn't mind talking about it, he just didn't want to **listen** about it!" The response—which I didn't think of at the time—is to challenge the person's inconsistency. Tell them that they are unfair to share and then to refuse to hear your response. Quit with the challenge, however, and change the topic of conversation. You will have your chance another day, and will be heard with a greater respect because of your assertiveness.

Along the same lines, it is wise to give the person an opportunity to "get off the hook."" After your initial try at bringing up the subject of your beliefs, look for an opportunity to change the subject to a non-religious topic—weather, sports, anything. Then if he doesn't bring it back to the religious topic within a short time, he wasn't interested. Again, if the topic doesn't come back, you've done your work for that day; wait for a new day to continue.

Another blockage to our witness may be that our friend feels he is meeting all of his life's needs. He may assume this proves that he has the right answers to the mysteries of life. He may also assume that if some other view were true, he would have already found it. Thus, since he has no current problems, his view of the world and its source must be correct. The answer to this smugness is a good discussion of the fact that he is "terminal." It's hard to be smug while discussing the sureness of death. Be careful, though! The tone of the discussion should be one of academic disinterest—not one of threat. He can draw the obvious conclusion without you having to fan the flames of hell beneath him.

You may also face an attitude of spiritual or mental superiority. The feeling of spiritual superiority is in every religion, but there is a double-dose in those who have been exposed to Rabbinic Judaism. (This comes from being viewed—by self and the world—as the parent of monotheism.) Second, Rabbinic Judaism teaches that if there is a life after death, Jewish people will be ushered into God's presence merely because they are Jewish. What insights could a Gentile have to offer?

The most common attempt to avoid an honest intellectual engagement is to try to ignore the whole thing. This is often done by assuming that you are a Christian out of ignorance or weakness. Obviously, it then behooves us to **not appear** ignorant or weak! If we do, these assumptions will become more entrenched with each assumed victory.

ATTITUDE CHECK!
Be self-assured,
but not arrogant!

Though the conviction of the gospel's truth is the job of the Holy Spirit, we are called to support that process by persuasion. In our part of the process, there is a psychological competition for power with our audience. To persuade, others must accept us as a teacher with skills or knowledge not held by them. No one receives instruction from another, unless he sees the person as the "expert" of the two. Put very bluntly, few Jewish people will ever listen to the religious views of anyone they think knows less about the God of Abraham than they do! (Again, the non-Jewish perception of the level of religious knowledge held by Jewish friends is highly exaggerated.)

Assuming a superior attitude, even when one is the expert, seems offensive to us. This comes from the value we place on modesty. However, this causes a problem. The Jewish community does not see modesty as a primary virtue. They live by the rule, "put your best foot forward." If we answer a question about religion by saying, "Well, I wouldn't presume to tell you about your religion....," they will assume we are ignorant and trying to avoid the question, not that we are a shy genius!

Paul gives the same strategy in Romans where he says, "I make much of my ministry (to the Gentiles) in the hope that I may somehow arouse my own people to envy and save some of them." Paul knew what he was talking about! Nothing gets Jewish attention better than a Christian who is more familiar with the God of Abraham than they are.

Remember, too, that we are planting in hard ground; don't fail to do a good job of plowing. That means we must break up old assumptions before new ideas will sprout. Practically speaking, we need to spend our initial witnessing sessions challenging the logic of current beliefs rather than by talking about ours. This calls for wisdom. We must walk right at the edge of being so blunt about the foolishness of our friend's views that we offend him–without crossing the line and doing so.

We also need to be a seed-sower and let the harvest wait until the grain is ripe. **Patience** must be the watchword! Initially, we must share our convictions without requiring any response to Jesus. We must be lovingly militant and repeatedly say by word and deed, "Once I was blind, but now I see!"

Chapter 12
THE START OF THE TRAIL

GOAL No. 1

*The discovery that God is a person, not an impersonal force. He is **CREATIVE**, **CONCERNED**, and **COMMUNICATIVE**.*

Charlie had Jewish classmates in high school, but none of them were among his close friends. As a young adult, he became a born-again believer. As the years passed he found that he walked in two worlds: a Christian world of Sunday worship and a secular world of work. Most of his fellow workers are Jewish; the rest are secular Gentiles. To the best of Charlie's knowledge, he is the only follower of Jesus in the firm.

As we eavesdrop on his conversations with his co-workers, perhaps we can learn how to lead our friends along the same path.

The initial task that Charlie faces with his Jewish friends—and that we face with ours—is to help them see God as a person, rather than an impersonal, detached force. We do this by showing three primary qualities of "personhood" in God.

God exercises these qualities, as the divine person, and shares them with us as human persons.

Here is a key concept to remember! When we say that God is a person, Jewish people assume that we are saying that God is a human being. Most Jewish people think of Jesus as a human whom Catholics deified, like the Romans deified their Caesars. They are amazed that we could believe that a man could become a god! Of course, no man can; but they have not yet considered that God could become a man.

This objection will be there, stated or not. If we answer it before it is raised, no one has to defend it. Here is how to do that. Any time you get into a discussion of religion, shift the conversation from talking about "wonderful people" to discussing what God must be like. Avoid topics like Mother Teresa or Gandhi–which is a direction your friend will choose to take–assuming he believes that doing good is the route to God. Let's listen to Charlie and Matt discuss this point.

"Matt–good to have you back from vacation. They've been working me to death; now they can work you to death for a while."

"It was great Charlie, to be out in the woods, get up early and make coffee over a fire outside the tent while everyone else was still asleep. You can't help but admire nature when you get away from the city for a while."

"What do you mean, nature?" asked Charlie.

"You know, creation, Mother Earth, the Force, whatever."

"You mean, God?"

"I guess so, whatever each person wants to call it. There has to be something bigger than us, some life force that surges through everything and energizes us all."

"You sound like everybody else," Charlie said. "Most people don't think of God as a person, but he is. In fact, we are persons—not because we are human, but because we have personality traits. These are traits of God that he has built into us—not human traits that we use to imagine God. For example, God is creative; so are we—in a smaller way. He hates injustice; so do we. He communicates; so do we. In fact, though no one can become a god, God could become a man to explain himself to us, if he chose to. After all, if there is a God, he can do anything he pleases, right?"

Stop here as Charlie and Matt go their way and finish their conversation. There are two important concepts, here. First, man is a copy of God, not vice versa. We are persons because we have been given qualities of the original person. Second, no man can become God, but God could become a man.

When it becomes clear that there is something outside of the machine of nature, Satan tries to portray God as a force, not a person. This limits religion to a search for moral principles, rather than a relationship with the Holy One.

Like the general population, most Jewish people believe "someone is out there." They believe it, not because they believe the Bible, but because it is a truth built in us.

We need to be alert to three different uses of the term "personal" and the three stages of intimacy reflected in them. Few Jewish people think it through, but most who do, think of Jehovah as their "personal God" in a sense of possessiveness. As the God of Israel, he belongs to them, rather than belonging to another community. There is no intimate involvement with God—which is the most important use of the term. He is just a part of what one owns as an element of his culture. Dealing with God as a person is foreign to most Jewish people.

Like most of the Jewish people, Matt believes—deep down—that we were created by some entity that he is willing to call god. He thinks, however, of that god as an "it" —as some sort of an undefined force. As far as how the world came to be, he has always assumed there was no answer other than evolution.

He certainly doesn't believe that this God communicates with humanity. Like most of his friends, he can't understand why such a God would be interested in an insignificant thing like an individual.

When we hear Charlie and Matt talk, we begin to recognize a pattern. Listen for the same pattern in your friend. People become philosophical, even though they don't recognize their philosophical framework. Questions eventually become, "Where did we come from and what is our destiny?" There is a sense, even with those that insist that we evolved, that we should somehow find God and spend eternity with him.

Where do they get those ideas, since few have ever opened a Jewish Bible, much less seen a New Testament? They come by God revealing himself as Creator through his creation, and the Holy Spirit pointing it out.[19] The theological term for this is "general revelation."

King David wrote, "The heavens declare the glory of God; the skies proclaim the work of his hands."[20] Jesus would later say, however, "...no one knows the Father except the Son and those to whom the Son chooses to reveal him."[21] General revelation can tell us that we need God, but it can't lead us to him.

---

[19] Romans 1:18-20.

[20] Psalm 19:1, NIV

[21] Matthew 11:27, NIV

Also, when the Holy Spirit works at this stage in the lives of people, he reminds them that their most basic need—safety and security—is still unmet. After all, until one solves the problem of death, he isn't really safe; and no one solves death for us except Jesus. Discussions of a hereafter spring from the fear of death. Don't avoid the subject! Avoid euphemisms like "passed on, just asleep on the hillside, resting," and others. The word is **dead.** If we try to water down the reality of death, we only lessen the sense of a need to overcome it.

When the questions of our beginning and end occur, what do we discuss? Basically, we talk about whatever our friend will hear. Also, until one is convinced of the truth of Genesis 1, that "In the beginning, God **created...**," it is counterproductive to try to convince him of John 1, "In the beginning was the Word...and the Word became flesh and dwelt among us."

Our affirmation that we were made by a Creator-God must be stated at whatever level we are allowed to work. To witness to God as Creator, we should have—already in our mind—three levels of response. These are (1) a non-Biblical statement showing the logic of believing there is a creator, (2) a Biblical verse that affirms it, and (3) an extended Bible study to support the verse, if interest develops.

TAKE NOTE!

Levels of needed response:

1. **Philosophical view**
2. **Biblical verse**
3. **Back-up study**

Since those at the beginning of the trail generally see the Bible as literature, **begin with logic rather than the Bible.** Remember though, the goal is always to get our friend into the scripture.

How do we use this with a friend who is musing on the question of the existence of a Supreme Being?

Be alert! You will need to know the following well enough to share it. Memorize it!

The best logic is the oldest. It is that **created things argue for a creator.** Since the world exists, we have two basic explanations for its existence from which to choose. We can believe in (1) an eternal creation that was self-generating, or (2) a Creator who originated it. Further, living in a world of order and **design calls for a designer.**

Another classic argument for a Creator God is that the very fact of **motion requires a prime (or initial) mover.** We live in a cause and effect world. This is very clear to the naturalist mindset, which—with rare exception—is the mindset of our Jewish friends. If one is intellectually consistent, he or she must seek the initial cause from which all observable effects spring. No matter how far your friend tries to go back through some sort of primal soup or big-bang theory, eventually he must take a stand on faith. He either stands, by faith, on the existence of an eternal Creator, or—by faith—on the eternal existence of a self-generated creation.

We can also argue that **everything reproduces itself.** Birds do not hatch minnows, nor do cows deliver colts. Equally true, chaos can not produce order, nor can anything uncreative, create. For example, how can we explain the source of man's creativity, except that it is the product of a greater creative person?

Evolution's followers propose that chaos and chance produced the intricate balance of nature. This is absurd to the uneducated—and is contrary to the scientific laws the educated claim to grasp! Most in the academic realms accept chance producing design because the only alternative is a Supreme Being. This is unacceptable to their philosophical prejudice.

Philosophy cannot prove or disprove the existence of God, but it is much more rational to believe in a pre-existent Creator than in a non-created creation. The words themselves scream against such foolishness. Philosophical support can be as extensive as you want. You can expand this from books on creationism written by Christian scientists and with those of religious philosophy, such as the works of Francis Schaeffer.

What then about Biblical response to the philosophical stand? What Biblical verse affirms the same truth that the logic establishes? It is Genesis 1:27, "So God created man in his own image. In the image of God, he created him; male and female he created them." **Memorize it!**

Genesis 1:27 affirms a designer for the design we see, a cause for observable effects, and a person who reproduced personhood in us. The best philosophical explanation of man is that his creativity, love, concern for justice, and appreciation for beauty, came from a greater source of the same qualities. This is also the Biblical claim. Thus, "man made in God's image" explains man's attributes of personhood.

God made man as a little model of himself, a miniature of his creativity as well as other qualities. If you share this truth, it will often produce an interest in finding out more of what the Bible tells us of man's origin. If so, then study Genesis together. (When this opportunity comes, select a self-study of Genesis from your church or a Christian book store. Get two copies, one for each of you. Using these and adding evangelistic insights is far better than trying to develop a study on your own. If you would like a good commentary on Genesis, consider *The Genesis Record,* by Henry M. Morris, who writes from a Biblical and scientific background.)

Again, making the case for a Creator God will not often be that difficult. If it is, become well enough versed on creationism to help your friend past this point. This is not a decision you can bypass. Objections more often come when we suggest that this God cares about us and is self-revealing.

EXPANDING GOAL No. 1:

*As a **person**, God is...*

1) creative,

2) concerned,

3) communicative.

*Thus, for a Jewish friend at the start of the trail, we must stress that God is (1) **creative**, (2) **concerned**, and (3) that he is **communicative**. We must not just show this in an academic way but must help him apply these truths. We must stay on this subject until our friend is convinced that:*

(1) God has created the human race in general and him specifically,

(2) that God communicates to mankind through the Bible, and that

(3) God's love for corporate humanity is merely the sum of his concern for each individual, including the friend to whom we are witnessing!

Chapter 13
THE CASE FOR A CONCERNED GOD

GOAL No. 2

To understand that the scripture is the authority through which we know of God and His love.

The Holy Spirit will increase our friend's desire to draw near to God. Again, just as we supported the truth that God made us, we must prepare to support the truth that God cares for individuals. Further we must show that this love implies contact by the one who loves us and that we have a record of his love letters. Let's eavesdrop on Charlie and Matthew and another discussion of God. Again, **become familiar with the logic given and memorize the scriptures.**

"Listen, Charlie, why should we expect God to care? The universe is a big place."

Trying to keep the emotional level at a low non-threatening point, Charlie waits a moment before he responds. "He cares because He created us. After all, we care about the things we make."

Matthew seems to relax and asks, "What do you mean?"

"Matt, what about your woodworking? Do you care less about a table because you have made more than one?"

"No."

"Well then, if you could make something as complex as a human being, don't you think you would care about it?"

That seems obvious to Matt. "Sure," he says. "We care about our children, which we create."

"Then why shouldn't we expect God to care about mankind, His greatest invention, and the individual children He has made? Where did we get that tendency to like what we make, even if it isn't alive? We got it from God's concern for what He made."

Seeing that Matt has caught his point, Charlie shifts the conversation from philosophical logic to the Biblical claim. "The Bible tells us that God does love us and is concerned about us. For example, the prophet Jeremiah records God's promise to always love the Jewish people, when God said, 'I have loved you with an everlasting love...'[22] David wrote of God's love by saying, 'The Lord will command his loving kindness in the daytime, and in the night his song shall be with me.'"[23]

Charlie then makes his last point. "Not only do we believe that God is loving, but we can know it—because He said so. God is self-revealing and the Scripture is the trustworthy record of that revelation."

Remember, for a Jewish friend, limit your claims of scriptural authority to the Old Testament for now. If you are asked, don't hesitate to say that you believe that the "Greek Scriptures" are God's revelation and that they confirm what the "Hebrew Scriptures" say. These are less offensive terms than the Old and the New Testaments—and are equally true. You can work out old and new covenant when your friend gets there. Don't try to do it this early.

---

[22] Jeremiah 31:3

[23] Psalms 42:8

As in dealing with creation, argue initially from logic until the scripture is accepted as God's word. The point to make is (1) that a loving God would want us to know Him, and (2) that we can't understand anything about God that He doesn't tell us.

LOGIC PROGRESSION!

1. A loving God would want us to know Him, and

2. all we can know of Him is what He tells us.

Any God who was worth our worship would be too hard for our puny brains to figure out! Again, we—God's model—want to communicate with those we love, therefore, we should expect the original—of which we are an image—to desire the same thing. Where then do we find God's love letters? The answer is obvious, it is in the record of God's movement in human history, the scriptures.

The point to convey is that we can't know anything about God by deduction—for we have no data from which to deduce. If He loves us—and we should expect His love—He should want us to know Him. For us to know Him, He must reveal Himself—since we have no knowledge of Him. If He moves in human history to reveal Himself, we need a record. That record of God's self-revelation in human history is the Scriptures. They are the **authority** on how to know God.

Our support role in this "first mile" is to assure our friend that weighing the potentiality of a Creator-God is mentally sound. Our friend should also see that if a God exists, it is reasonable to expect God to be aware of him and want to reach him. Our stress on God's interest should be balanced between the fact that God loves us and that He holds us responsible for what we do. One of the best illustrations of this balance is to show that God held Adam and Eve responsible for their disobedience, but in love sought them out and made a way of return for them into His presence. If so, the study of Genesis 3 is critical. For the points to be covered, see the Appendix.

As you begin to establish your claim that God loves us and that the Bible says so, a natural resistance to trusting the Bible will surface. Most likely, it won't be an argumentative position but the testing of a new idea.

Hopefully, your friend will have come to the place of accepting the need for God to reveal Himself. Still, he may need encouragement to see the Bible as a trustworthy history of that revelation. If so, you will need to give him some background on how we got the Bible. If you need a resource, *Evidence that Demands a Verdict* is a good one.

A helpful scripture to review is Isaiah 48:8-10 (see Appendix for background commentary.) The point is that the proof of whose God was the real god was Israel's ability to witness (display a record) of God's fulfilled prophecy in their midst. Capacity to foretell the future without any error is the proof of the validity of Israel's God.

Hopefully your friend will move up the trail to the next check point. You will have succeeded in completing the first mile, if your "Matthew" is willing to discuss God with you and has moved to the point where he (1) believes God to be a person, not a force; (2) believes that he is God's deliberate creation; and (3) that the Bible is a trustworthy record of God's self-revelation.

Chapter 14
YOM KIPPUR, TODAY

Yom Kippur, or the Day of Atonement, is a universal holy day in the Jewish community. Even assimilated Jews will try to find a way to attend synagogue on this day. The few who do not attend will spend the day thinking about it.

Synagogues that are otherwise virtually empty will be overflowing; seating is by reservation. Most who attend will understand little of the liturgy and less of its Biblical base, but they will feel compelled to attend.

Since Yom Kippur is so central to the community's sense of Jewishness, being familiar with its Rabbinic practice—as well as the Biblical requirements is a basic necessity.

The new year begins the "Yamim Noraim" or the Days of Awe. These ten days form a unit, beginning with Rosh Hashanah, the Jewish New Year, and ending in a 24-hour fast on Yom Kippur, the Day of Atonement.

Though few of your Jewish friends will observe all of the "Days of Awe," it is useful to know the Orthodox practice for these High Holy Days. Members of Reform or Conservative synagogues follow the same pattern, but are less stringent than the Orthodox. Those who are nominally religious—which most of your friends will be—will do bits and pieces of the process.

What then is involved in the current celebration of Yom Kippur? In Elud, the last month in the Jewish calendar (mid-August to mid-September,) the rabbis begin to stress the coming time of repentance. They sound the shofar, or ram's horn, as a part of the synagogue services to spiritually awaken the people. This calls them to an alertness for the coming days. The shofar also acts as a reminder of the sacrifice of Isaac, which will be the scripture reading for Rosh Hashanah, New Year's day. It also reminds them of the gift of the Law on Mount Sinai.

Synagogue prayer services in the last month of the year include a confession of sins, prayed in unison as a penitential prayer, and the recitation of the 13 attributes of God.

In the weeks preceding the new year, friends greet each other with "Ketivah Ve'Chatimah Tovah." This means, "May you be inscribed and sealed for a good year." The proper response is, "Gam Atem," which means, "The same to you."

Loved ones who have died are remembered during this time. Many Jewish families visit the cemetery as a part of the season. Some take prayer books and recite prayers for the dead. Others just take their memories and meditate on the good times once shared with the person buried there.

Because the year begins with a spiritual cleansing, a good house cleaning is also part of the season's preparation. Also, the family buys new clothes for the synagogue services.

The season has its special foods. The challah, a special Jewish braided ceremonial bread, is now baked in a circle, rather than a long loaf. Its circle signifies a desire for life to continue for the coming year in its unending cycle. Honey, honey cakes, and fresh apples are a part of Rosh Hashanah, or the New Year's celebration. They reflect the wish for a "sweet" and prosperous year ahead.

As the year begins, the rabbis stress "teshuvah," which is Hebrew for repentance. They consider repentance to be a perpetual task, but heighten its emphasis at this season.

The "Hatarat Nedarim"—the Days of Awe—stress **man's capacity** to forgive sins against fellow man and against God. Just before Rosh Hashanah, the first day of the ten day season of repentance, the men of the community gather in groups of four. One asks the other three to release him from any religious obligations to God or man, that he may not have completed. The other three become a "bet din," or a court of law, to grant him absolution. They then rotate until they annul the unfulfilled promises of each.

The first day, Rosh Hashanah, begins with the evening meal. It is much like the Sabbath meal, except the blessing of the children is for the coming year.

In the morning synagogue service, the scripture reading is of the sacrifice of Isaac. The Shofar is blown and special prayers are recited.

That afternoon, some families practice "Tashlich." In Hebrew, this means, "you shall cast." They go to the sea or some running water, such as a river, and cast bread symbolizing their sins into the water. They see these as being cast away, never to return. The roots of this are in Micah 7:19. It reads, "You will again have compassion on us; you will tread our sins underfoot and hurl all our iniquities into the depths of the sea."

On the day before Yom Kippur, the last day of the Days of Awe, some of the more orthodox still practice "Kapparot." In this, the father brings home a live chicken, twirls it by the neck over each member of the household, and says, "This is in exchange for you. This is your atonement. This chicken will go to death, but you will go on to a good and long life and to peace."[24] Then he takes the chicken to a kosher butcher, has it killed and given to the poor. This way, it does double duty; it provides atonement plus a "mitszvot," or merit from a good deed. Those who are more modern use money instead of a chicken and give the money to their favorite charity. The obvious basis of this practice is the scape goat of Leviticus 16, which was led into the wilderness after the sins of the people were laid upon it.

The ten day season of repentance ends with a 24-hour fast on Yom Kippur. An early evening meal precedes this day of fasting. The fast begins as the people walk to synagogue, just prior to sundown, for the evening service. They dress in white, to show purity and innocence. The Orthodox wear a "kittel," a white robe, over their new suits. Gold isn't worn, lest it remind God of Israel's sin with the golden calf. With this fine dress, the standard shoes are tennis shoes. This is because leather comes from a dead animal and would have made one ceremoniously unclean.

Some of the other prohibitions of the fast day, other than leather shoes, include more obvious things. One may not work, eat, nor drink water on this fast day. Sex and bathing are prohibited.

During the evening services, and those of the coming day, the people focus on confession of sins. They confess, corporately and in unison, forty-four categories of sin. At the final service, they close by praying "Next Year in Jerusalem."

---

[24] Blu Greenberg, *How to Run a Traditional Jewish Household* (New York: Simon and Schuster, Inc., 1983), p. 334.

Chapter 15
YOM KIPPUR AND THE NEED OF ATONEMENT

GOAL No. 3

To know that "without the shedding of blood, there is no redemption."

The Biblical requirement for Yom Kippur, or the Day of Atonement, is given in Leviticus 16, but the atonement process was well established before Sinai. It began at the gate of Eden with the sacrifice of the animals for the skins God used to cloth Adam and Eve. After man brought death into the world by disregarding God's warning, God made a way for humanity to "visit" his presence through a sacrificial system involving the shedding of blood.

Ministers need to correct a major misuse of the word, atonement. It literally means "to cover." Many use the term "atonement" for the sacrifice of Jesus on the cross, but Jesus did much more than "cover" our sins; he removed them from existence. Some of the modern translations make this mistake, and in this case, the old is better than the new. The King James version correctly uses the term "propitiation," which means to conciliate an offended divine power.

Human beings could come into God's presence, on a temporary basis, when they had their sins covered, or "atoned." This "cover" provided an entry for worship, but did not change the fact that the worshiper's life was temporary—that is, limited to a physical, terminal, span of time.

The Old Testament sacrificial system gave no one eternal life. Observing the Law "saved" no one according to Hebrews 10. All are given eternal life through the "propitiation" of Jesus the Messiah. (Man's part—Abraham, Moses, Paul, you and me—in being made right with God, has always been to trust, that is, exercise faith. The classic statement of this is the source of Abraham's righteous stand before God. It did not come by any action such as keeping the Law, but by God's grace because of Abraham's trust.)[25] We are saved through the Messiah's conciliation of our offended Creator. Atonement was a temporary resolution to the problem of man's sins until God-the-Son would come with the permanent solution.

Think of it this way; atonement was the lid on our garbage can, which "covered" our sins so we could worship God. However, Jesus became our trash-truck and permanently hauled them away to Hell's dumping ground. Now, we have a permanent, or eternal entry into God's presence—not with our sins covered (atoned,) but gone. Praise God!

Leviticus, chapter 16, gives the Biblical requirements for Yom Kippur. The process had three stages, which we find fulfilled in Christ's death on the cross. They were: (1) what must be done to enter God's presence in order to deal with the problem of sin, (2) the removal of the offending sins, and (3) the just payment for Israel's times of deliberate disobedience.

---

[25] Genesis 15:6

God gave the instruction for Yom Kippur after he killed two of Aaron's sons because of their presumption. God tells Moses that even the High Priest, Aaron, may not come into The Holy of Holies, the center of the Tabernacle, whenever he chooses. When he enters, even to fulfill his priestly duty, he must do so under the protection of a set ritual. Thus, Aaron could only enter with the proper protective covering, or to quote God, "he would die."

Again, the first step in the national atonement on Yom Kippur was for Aaron to enter God's presence to offer the atoning blood, without dying. To enter, Aaron had to bathe, dress in special clothing, and make an offering for himself. Physically clean and with his sins covered, he could then intercede for the people of Israel.

Leviticus 4 describes the sin offering, which God required for people's unintentional sins. The first barrier to man's redemption is not his deliberate breaking of God's laws, but his fallen nature. We rarely show this side of human lostness, but it springs from our not being what God created us to be; perfect people. Paul would later maintain that we are cut off, even without breaking a commandment. He writes that death, which came by sin, existed before the Law was given. Thus, Aaron could not enter God's presence to deal with Israel's disobedience until atonement was made for fallen human nature.

Gaining entry into God's presence, Aaron, as High Priest, could move to the next step. This required two goats that formed a unit. One goat would become the sin offering for the people. It covered their fallen nature—their unintentional sins. The other goat would provide for the removal of Israel's sins from their presence. This second step, the removal of sins from the people, left only one thing for the atonement to be complete, the burnt offering.

Aaron took these two goats, brought for the whole community, and presented them to God at the entrance of the Tabernacle. By casting lots, he selected which would be sacrificed and which would be set free.

In offering the people's sin offering, God told Aaron to bring the goat to the tent doorway and to place his hands on its head, confessing Israel's sins over it. This laying on of hands and confession placed the sins of the people on the goat. It was then led away, with the sins of the people, and released in the wilderness. This second part of Yom Kippur was completed as the second goat became the vehicle for the removal of Israel's sins.

The problem of man's imperfection, not being what he was created to be, was covered. Aaron had gained entry into God's presence by the blood of the offering for fallen human nature. So too, the specific incorrect actions of Israel, their sins, were removed. The scape goat had carried Israel's sins away. What, though, of the deliberate attitude of disobedience? That sacrifice still remained to be made. Last, Aaron offers his and the people's burnt offering to complete their atonement.

At this point, Aaron shifts from functioning as a priest on behalf of the people to participating with them. He bathes again and redresses in his regular clothes. He then makes his burnt offering with the rest of Israel.

Many commentaries miss the meaning of the burnt offering because its specific purpose is not stated. We are given the meanings of the sin offering and guilt offering, however. The writer assumes his readers already know the purpose of the oldest of the Biblical sacrifices.

We find the key to the purpose of the Burnt Offering in Leviticus 7:8 in a unique fact. It is that the hide of the burnt offering is the property of the priest to do with as he chooses.

The priest being given the hide to use as he chooses reminds all of the first burnt offering. Then, God, as the priest, used the hide to cover (atone for) the sins of deliberate disobedience of God's direct command by Adam and Eve. (They did not need to cover their physical nakedness, but "atone"—cover—their sins.) Thus the last act of Yom Kippur—the Burnt Offering—was a sacrifice to cover Aaron's and Israel's deliberate breaking of God's commands. It was for deliberate known disobedience.

What does this teach, or foretell? The whole Levitical worship system is fulfilled in Jesus, the Messiah, as the ultimate solution to man's separation from God. Hebrews 9 and 10 discuss this and should be read and re-read until they are familiar passages. We must convince our Jewish friends of the following:

KEY INSIGHTS TO SHARE!

1. Necessity of blood sacrifice
2. Man can't change God's requirements
3. First Problem to solve? Attitude, not actions!
4. Completion requires an individual choice.

1. Entry into God's presence only comes by the sacrifice of blood. Current Rabbinic Judaism has substituted other things, but the scripture is very clear. Leviticus 17:11 says, "...it is the blood that makes an atonement for your souls."

2. God, not man, sets the standards by which we are redeemed. Aaron's sons died because of presumption! Their mistake was thinking they could choose to vary God's sacrificial instructions. Current Rabbinic substitution of prayer, fasting, and good deeds is no more authorized than the changes that cost Nadab and Abihu their lives.

Jesus would make the same point. He would talk about the narrow way that leads to eternal life. It has always been narrow; in fact, there is only one way, God's way.

3. Man's initial problem to solve is not his wrong actions, but his wrong attitude. Yom Kippur began with a covering of the sins of an imperfect nature—unintentional infractions covered by sin offering.

The two goats form a unit that teaches two halves of the salvation process. Entry into God's presence to deal with the problem came by blood, but entry only brought an opportunity to solve the problem. The other half is that sins must be removed. This was the function of the second goat. So far the process of atonement was universal for all.

So too, Jesus, as the eternal High Priest, entered God's judicial chambers by his own blood. He also carried mankind's sinful acts away permanently, just as the scape goat removed Israel's sins, temporarily.

4. The last sacrifice, the burnt offering, was payment for deliberate disobedience. Aaron did not officiate during the burnt offerings as a priest, but as an individual person with the balance of the nation. This is why he was required to redress in his regular clothes. When the offerings for deliberate disobedience were made, each person—including Aaron—stood before God as an individual.

Jesus is our burnt offering for deliberate rebellion as well as the sin offering for our imperfection. In Yom Kippur's fulfillment in Jesus, we face a requirement that is clearly stated in the New Testament and implied in the pattern. It is that we must make a deliberate choice of trusting Jesus' sacrifice to pay for our rebellion for it to be effective. This final element of forgiveness is not automatic for everyone on the earth, but comes with individual trust.

Chapter 16
USING YOM KIPPUR IN EVANGELISM

First, let's do a quick review. We have moved up the trail and are at the third check-point. Earlier check-points were: 1) to believe that God is a **PERSON**, and as our **CREATOR**, is **CARING**, and **COMMUNICATES** his concern and 2) we have a trustworthy record of God's self-revelation. The scripture is the authority on what God requires and seeks in us.

The check-point currently under discussion is that God is a redeeming God, and that **REDEMPTION IS–AND HAS ALWAYS BEEN–BY SACRIFICIAL BLOOD.** No revisions allowed!

Initially, everyone assumes that he is going to heaven–if a heaven exists. Man is so egotistical that he can see himself as "good enough," even if he is on death-row and knows he is guilty. Humans have an endless capacity to rationalize away their responsibility for sin.

Don't be surprised at this stage if your friend suggests there may be other ways to heaven. When faced with salvation by grace, almost everyone tries to find another way to God. Here you must show that the way of return to God must be found and that how we get there is God's option, not ours. If you can show that whatever avenue of return must have the elements mandated in Biblical atonement, eventually Jesus becomes the only answer.

We also reverse our emphasis at this stage. Before the scripture was accepted as God's word, the major emphasis was philosophical logic supported by scripture. Now, we reverse these. Scripture becomes the major emphasis, with logic taking a supporting role.

If our friend is not open to accept the Bible as the authority of God's self-revelation, don't work on any other point until this is accomplished. Don't go on down the trail if your friend is stuck.

Witnessing at this point may be limited to general conversation. If that's your only opportunity, talk about Yom Kippur, its current practice and its Biblical basis. If you can, share a Bible study of Leviticus 16 and review the same things.

The obvious time to bring this up is following Yom Kippur. You don't have to wait, however, if you have a friend ready to move on up the trail. To get the feeling of this, let's eavesdrop again on Charlie and Matthew as they begin their day.

Charlie parked the car in his slot at work and stepped out to lock it. It was a bright fall morning with the trees changing colors around the company parking lot. You could see God's hand, even in the midst of this concrete and steel world. Matthew had just parked and came by Charlie as he turned to walk toward the warehouse.

"Morning, Matt," said Charlie, "We missed you, yesterday. Almost no one was here. Did you go to synagogue or did you play hooky?"

"I was in synagogue. I even went to an Orthodox service, which was long and boring, but it felt good to attend."

"Does your family do the thing with the chicken?"

Matt was puzzled. "What are you talking about?" he asked.

Trying to appear detached, Charlie said, "It's a Jewish custom where the father brings home a live chicken, swings it over each family-member's head and says, 'This chicken is for your atonement. It will die for your sins, but you will live.' Then it's killed and given to the poor."

"Be serious, Charlie. I've never heard of that."

"No, it's true, I read about it in a book. It's a very common thing in the older, more Orthodox communities. This book said that, today, some people use money instead of a chicken and then give the money to the poor. They get this from the Biblical instructions for the Day of Atonement. You can read it for yourself?"

Charlie's suggestion left Matt incredulous. "Are you kidding?" he said. "Even the rabbis don't understand the Talmud. How do you expect me to get through it?"

Charlie picked-up on Matt's unconscious shift. "I'm not talking about the Talmud," he said. "I'm talking about the Bible. That's what the Talmud is supposed to be based on. Look, Matt, good research never looks at secondary findings if the original data is available. The Bible is the original data and it isn't that hard. Come by at lunch and I'll let you read the original instructions."

"OK—see you then."

Charlie's object—and ours—is to get Matt into the scripture and to show that redemption only comes through blood. You can start such a conversation by simply asking about Yom Kippur and then moving from there. The question about Kapparot, the atonement chicken or money, is important because it draws the person closer to the truth of atonement by blood than the stress on prayers, fasting, and repentance. The latter are human acts, and as such, have no place in atonement.

The comment, "... good research never looks at secondary findings if the original data is available." is a phrase that ought to be **memorized** and used repeatedly. Jewish friends will look to the Talmud as the authority for religious truth, though they have no idea what it says. We must show that the religious authority for their lives is not the Talmud, but the scripture. Shocking as it may be to Christians, much of the Talmud disagrees with the Old Testament.

When the discussion turns to Yom Kippur, or hopefully, when you study Leviticus 16 together, the general pattern should be to question your "Matt" as to why he attended and what it did for him. The general response is that it brings forgiveness of sins. If he says this, turn the conversation to why we need forgiveness. He will think we need absolution because we are unethical in dealing with each other. We must guide him to perceiving it as necessary to make us right with God. The authority to declare that it is to make us right with God, rather than fellow man, is Leviticus 16.

In a study or discussion, we should affirm that the God of Leviticus is very dogmatic in his instructions. In fact, to fail in any minute point was to die! If God is that exact, what right do we have to change the rules? If God says, in Leviticus 17:11—which you should memorize—"For a creature's life is in its blood, and I have given it to you upon the altar to make an atonement for your lives; **it is the blood that makes atonement for you**," then man's works of fasting, repentance, and prayers won't atone! (If your friend has checked with his rabbi, he may bring up passages where God rejects Israel's sacrifices as an evaluation away from a requirement to shed blood. A major one is Micah 6:8, "He has shown you, O man, what is good. What does the LORD require of you but to act justly, love mercy, and walk humbly before him?" If this or some other passage is presented, review it together within the whole passage. In context, you will see it does not justify rabbinic substitution.)

Don't lose sight of the purpose of the discussion. It is to convince him that Rabbinic Judaism's answer doesn't work. Don't muddy that by trying to make your case for Christianity; it's too early. Your Matt will wonder in his mind, and may even ask, "What about you? Christian's don't do this either. You don't follow these rules."

Our response should be that Rabbinic requirements of prayer, fasting, and repentance are good, but don't atone. Kapparot, the killing of the chicken, comes closer but isn't what the scripture mandates. Our response should be, "The message is that atonement comes by blood. Our hope is in the blood of Jesus, where's your hope?" We don't have to convince our friend that this is valid at this point. He will only come to hope in the Messiah when he gives up on all other avenues. After he thrashes around awhile in the underbrush looking for another trail, we can come back and help him. Then he can move on up the path to the decision that Jesus is not just a way but the only way.

Chapter 17
THE BIBLICAL PASSOVER

If Yom Kippur is the Jewish community's most universal holy day, Pesach, or "Passover," is second. These two holidays form the total observance for most Jewish families. Even then, the level of observance will vary. For many, it is merely a family gathering—like Christmas dinner for cultural Christians. For the practicing few, "Pesach," or Passover is primarily a time to instruct the young and cement traditions. For them, the meal is secondary.

Most Christians are familiar with Passover and herein lies the danger. Being on familiar ground, the Christian is prone to jump ahead of his Jewish colleague and assume Jewish people see what Christians see in the Exodus. Christians correctly see God reclaiming the Jewish people for himself and for his purposes. Jewish friends don't see that. They see a Jewish escape from slavery into self-determination.

The word "Passover" means two different things to born-again Christians and their Jewish friends. Anyone who grew up in Sunday School will automatically think of the Death Angel "passing over" those protected by the blood. Jewish friends will think of family gatherings they enjoyed as children. Worse, each group is unaware of the mental picture that "Passover" brings to the other.

The first chapter of Exodus records the historic event. The Jewish life described in Exodus is radically different from the life of Jacob and his sons at the end of Genesis. At the death of Joseph, they are a family of privilege in Egypt. Sixty-four years later, at the birth of Moses, they are a nation of slaves. Most explanations of the change hinge on the human conditions. Investigators sift the dust of archeological sites for details behind the ominous verse that says, "Then a new king who did not know Joseph came into power."

In the human history between Joseph and Moses, Egypt fell to an outside invasion of the Hyksos, the shepherd kings. A major view is that when the Egyptian dynasty fell, so did its friends. Others place the dates of the various Egyptian dynasties at different times (no one knows for sure) and believe that Israel was enslaved after the shepherd kings were displaced.

Ezekiel gives us the reason for Israel's enslavement. The changing political tides of Egypt were only God's tool, not the cause of Israel's downfall. In Ezekiel 20:8, God gives the reason **he** enslaved them. It was an expression of wrath for their idolatry with the gods of Egypt.

When Moses returned to Egypt, redemption was not the hope of Israel. Their hope was to be reinstated to privilege while remaining in Egypt. Their concept of a deliverer was one who would help them recover their previous position. The rebellion Moses faced is easier to understand when we realize that a trip into the desert was not what Israel had in mind.

To move, Israel had to be motivated in two directions. First, if living conditions had not been as harsh as they were, Israel would not have left. Second, since the idolatry of Egypt dominated their lives, they needed as much convincing that Jehovah was the true God as their Egyptian masters.

The plagues not only impressed the Hebrew slaves with Jehovah's power, but impressed many others as well. The estimated two million who made the Exodus are described as a "mixed multitude." Surely every slave in Egypt, whether Hebrew, Canaanite, or Phoenician, left when the escape opportunity came. Secondly, many who were not slaves followed the God of the Hebrews because of the miracles.

Early in today's Passover Seder (the "order" of the meal) the Plagues are recited and remembered. As the father of the home mentions the individual plagues, each person dips his finger in his wine and drops a drop of wine to remember that plague. This spilled wine symbolizes a hint of sadness among the joy—a sadness for the Egyptian suffering caused by their leader's hard-headedness.

The plagues were progressive in their severity and were basically an attack of the individual Egyptian gods. The first eight form two sets, one from the Nile and one from the land. The ninth plague is a time of darkness and the tenth the death of the first born.

The water-born plagues begin with the Nile turning to blood. They continue with frogs, mosquitoes (sometimes translated as gnats or lice,) and water beetles (sometimes translated as flies.) Egypt viewed the Nile as its chief deity. They saw it as the source of all life. It was the ancient "primordial soup" from which all things sprang. Frogs were the "sacred cows" of ancient Egyptian religion. They could not be deliberately killed or hampered in any way. The mosquitoes were a very annoying form of life for "mother Nile" to produce. The fourth may have been the Scarab beetle, which was also a worship object.

Of these first four, Israel suffered with the Egyptians under the first three. The fourth, the beetles (or flies) were not a problem in Goshen.

The price of resistance increased with the land plagues. Goshen, however, continued to be exempt. The first land plague was a cattle disease, which symbolically struck at the sacred bulls of Egyptian idolatry. Next came boils, which brought anguish to the people. A hail storm followed, destroying the crops and killing every living thing left outside. God warned them, however, and those who took him seriously protected their cattle and slaves. Last, when the crops came up again, locusts arrived and ate them.

The ninth and tenth plagues were the final exhibit of Jehovah's power over the false gods of Egypt. The sun was blotted out for three days. The only light that existed was in the land of Goshen. The tenth condemned the view that the Pharaoh was a god. It showed that he could not protect his house from death any better than the lowest of his slaves.

Most of the time we only remember the tenth plague, but the Passover story continues through the crossing of the Red Sea. When they crossed the Red Sea, Israel was not free to practice self-determination. Ceasing to be the slaves of Egypt, they became the possession of God. Like Israel, we are not saved for our own self-determination. We too, are redeemed from the slavery of Satan to become what we were destined to be—God's possessions. Like Israel, we gain a new identity because we are new people.

Chapter 18
PASSOVER, TODAY AND IN JESUS' DAY

Today's Passover Seder is a modification of the Biblical requirements given in Exodus and Leviticus. Today, three holidays are celebrated as one. Biblically, these are Passover, Unleavened Bread, and the Feast of First Fruits.

The actual Passover is eaten as an evening meal on the fourteenth of Nisan, a Jewish month falls in March or April on our Roman calendar. It is the reenactment of the meal Israel ate as they prepared to leave Egypt. The elements required by the Bible are a roasted lamb, bread without any yeast, and bitter herbs.

Tradition has replaced the lamb and added some other items, because the temple is not available for sacrifice. A shank bone symbolizes the lamb. Though there are a variety of traditional foods, the meal substituted for the lamb can be anything the family enjoys. It should, of course, be kosher and without yeast. The unleavened bread and bitter herbs are still a part of the ritual.

Those who observe the full eight day period continue abstaining from any food that contains yeast for an additional week. The first and last days of this week are Sabbaths, or days of rest. This week of Unleavened Bread—immediately following Passover—is a time of consecration to God.

Another Biblical holiday falls at the same time. It is the Feast of First Fruits. In early Israel, its uniqueness was in its tie to the Barley harvest and its requirement to always fall on Sunday. Israel celebrated First Fruits as soon after Passover as the Barley was ready to harvest.

All of these holidays were fulfilled in the death of Jesus. He fulfilled Passover in his death, Unleavened Bread in his consecration to God unto death, and First Fruits by his resurrection on Sunday. He not only fulfilled the teaching of these feasts, but he also fulfilled their exact calendar. He celebrated Passover with his men on the evening of 14 Nisan and died on Passover day. He was raised on Sunday, fulfilling First Fruits. God is very exact in his dates and times.

The Passover that Jesus celebrated was similar to the traditional Pesach Seder of today. Today's Seder (the order of events) begins with a teaching time using the symbolic foods and remembering the Exodus. Following this initial time of remembrance, the family has the actual meal. Last, there is an additional teaching time and the Passover is complete.

The symbolic foods consist of four cups of wine, matzah (unleavened bread), and a central Seder plate with seven items on it. These are symbolic and separate from the actual meal. Since there are set rituals to perform, Christians are prone to expect a tone of awe. Yet, the ritual is not a thing of "magic." It is a teaching tool, being passed from generation to generation.

The order of the events begins as the host pronounces the "Kiddish," the blessing over the first cup of wine. Though most will say the blessing in Hebrew, it is translated, "Blessed art Thou, O Lord, King of the Universe, Creator of the fruit of the vine." Everyone then drinks the first cup of wine, which is the Cup of Sanctification. It is to express one's commitment to God.

After reciting additional blessings, the host—and in some cases everyone—ceremoniously washes his hands. Most likely, it was at this point in the Seder that Jesus washed the feet of his disciples. If so, he turned what was a high honor into a teaching of humility.

Following the ceremonial hand washing, the host takes a bit of Parsley for each guest from the central Seder plate. He dips it in the salt water and shares it with them. The parsley dipped in salt water reminds us of the hyssop dipped in blood and sprinkled on the doorposts that night, long ago. It also reminds us of the tears of affliction Israel suffered as slaves.

Next, the host turns everyone's attention to the matzah, which is kept in a special pouch. On the outside this pouch resembles a small decorated pillowcase. Inside, it has three compartments. Each compartment holds a matzot, though the three matzot are considered a single unit.

Now, the center matzot, called the Bread of Affliction, is removed and broken. The larger part is wrapped in a napkin and hidden away. It will be recovered at the end of the meal.

The source of considering the three matzot as one, and the breaking and hiding of the center one is lost in antiquity. The practice developed following the loss of the Temple, but no one knows the exact details. Another interesting factor is that in the early years following the loss of the temple, this hidden portion—called the Aphikoman—became a symbol of the Messiah.

The most plausible explanation is that these views came from the early Jewish church. No Jewish believer would ever again practice the Passover without including the Lord's Supper, just as Jesus did on the night he was betrayed. Though current Rabbinic leadership tries to discount the influence of the early church on Jewish life, it was a significant force.

If Jesus was the source of this practice, the "burial" of this broken bread of affliction and its "resurrection" make a perfect picture of his death. The fact that it is the center matzot seems symbolic as well. Sadly, the Jewish community has had this witness in its midst for centuries and missed it.

After the hiding of the Aphikoman, the story of the plagues and the exodus is shared. Next the other elements on the central Seder plate are explained and shared.

There are five elements, in addition to the parsley and salt water used earlier. The "Z'roah" is a lamb's shankbone and represents the Passover Lamb. Next to it is a roasted egg representing the sacrifices given during the Week of Unleavened Bread following Passover.

The Bitter Herbs takes two forms. One dish is horseradish; the other is the "Karpus." This is generally parsley, but it may also be a vegetable, such as an onion or boiled potato. This and the horseradish represent the bitterness of slavery.

Last, there is "Charoset" which is a mixture of chopped apples, walnuts, and wine made to represent the mortar.

Following this review of life in Egypt's slavery and God's blessings in delivering Israel, each person drinks the second cup of wine, the Cup of Thanksgiving.

In the more Orthodox homes, one final act closes the initial teaching session. The host prepares a tiny sandwich for each guest. The first and third matzot, broken into small pieces, provides the bread for these. A portion of each, with a piece of the bitter herbs, make this symbolic meal. Before the loss of the temple, a small piece of lamb was included. This tiny symbolic sandwich is the "sop" that Jesus gave to Judas just before he left on his mission of betrayal.

After sharing this symbolic Passover meal, the teaching portion is interrupted with the actual meal. When the dinner is completed, the Passover ritual continues with the remaining two cups of wine and the Aphikoman, the broken matzot that has been hidden during the meal. The father encourages the children to find the hidden matzot. The one who finds it gets a prize. It is then broken into small pieces and shared with each participant. The participants stand and the host leads them in prayers. These are blessings of God for his goodness to Israel. Each then takes the third cup, the Cup of Redemption, and drinks it.

The hidden matzot and the Cup of Redemption are the elements Jesus used to institute the Lord's Supper. Luke shows us it was this Cup of Redemption that Jesus shared, when he says, "...after the supper he took the cup (the cup following the actual meal is the Cup of Redemption,) saying, 'This is the new covenant in my blood, which is poured out for you."

The host then pours each a fourth cup of wine, the Cup of Completion. He recites the prayers of praise and each drinks his last cup of wine. The Seder is then closed with a final prayer.

Chapter 19
PASSOVER AND EVANGELISM

GOAL No. 4

To see the Messiah as God's Passover Lamb, the source of shed blood protecting us from spiritual death.

Again, review where we are in the process. To begin one must believe that **GOD IS CREATOR**, and thus **CARING**. Second, if God is caring, we should expect him to **COMMUNICATE** his love. The Bible is our record of God's self-revelation. Third, one must believe that **REDEMPTION IS—AND HAS ALWAYS BEEN—BY SACRIFICIAL BLOOD**. Now, one must see **JESUS AS GOD'S PERFECT SACRIFICE** to save, **perfectly**.

The key to any evangelistic discussion about Passover is to get out of the memories of the Seder and its accompanying meal, and into the scripture. If your "Matt" will join you, study Exodus 11:1-12:13 and Matthew 26:17-28:15 together. If not, know this material well, so you can share it in full detail from memory. If you meet for Bible study, take a Bible for your friend; most likely, he won't have one. In fact, buy an inexpensive paperback Bible, encourage him to make notes in it, and give it to him for his study.

As you study together, it is a good idea to go through one book at a time, noting the main points of the material. Don't move back and forth between Exodus and Matthew; it will cause confusion. Also, don't spend time on details that don't support your main purpose, which is to show Jesus as the way of redemption.

The first point to make—and write on paper as you study together—is from Exodus 12. (Why not get your Bible and read it as you go through the following material?) When judgment came, what protected Israel? Exodus 12:1-13 answers this. From these verses you should draw the conclusion that only those who trusted in the blood of the lamb were saved. Everyone else faced the death angel. Also, that being Jewish didn't save anyone; the blood did. Nor did being Egyptian condemn anyone; the lack of the protective blood did. If an Israelite rejected God's way of redemption, death struck; if an Egyptian trusted God's way, the angel "passed over."

Last, everyone had a choice as to his response to God's command. The night of Passover brought either judgment or redemption. No family was exempt. All, by their choice faced life or death.

Let's review. The study of the original Passover in Exodus 11:1-12:13 should cause your "student" to agree with the following conclusions:

1. Protection was provided by God through the blood of the passover lamb.

2. Passover brought redemption or judgment, dependent on each household's choice.

Now turn to Matthew 26:17-28:15. You may need to give some background to bring your friend up to the point of the story. He may know nothing about Jesus.

If he does he may believe him to be a good man whom the early Roman Catholics deified. He will believe that you and other current Christians just adopted their myth like children adopt the myth of Santa Claus. This is the time to repeat, "No man can become a god, but God could become a man if he wanted to." The question you must make him face is whether God did or not. Let's follow Charlie and Matt as they study Matthew 26:17 through 28:15.

"Now turn to the book of Matthew," says Charlie. "That's about two-thirds of the way through the Bible, but its easier to check the index, like we did for Leviticus."

"Here it is, page 1289."

"OK, Matt, we have the same thing I was showing you in the other books. Here, too, the books are broken down into chapters—that's the big numbers—and the chapters are broken down into verses. The verses are all the same, no matter what Bible you have, but all Bibles don't have the paragraphs. By the way, all of this—the chapters and verses—were not a part of what Moses or Matthew wrote. Scholars added these later so people could all find the same place more quickly."

(You may think no one would need this instruction, but non-Christians will. If you tell them how to find a reference quickly, without making it seem odd that they don't know how, you can help them save face.)

"Have you found it?"

"Yes," says Matt.

"OK, then turn to chapter 26 and find verse 17. You can follow the chapter numbers at the top—like a dictionary."

"I've got it."

"Matt, hold your place, and let's get some background. What did we learn from the two holidays we studied in the Hebrew scripture?"

"That God saved Israel because they marked their houses with blood."

"Right, and what principles should they have learned from that? What does it teach us?"

"Well, they were either saved or doomed by whether they put the blood on their doors. I guess it resembled the blood of Yom Kippur. Somehow the blood was God's requirement for them to be spared. But Charlie, I don't see what that's got to do with us. We don't face any death angel."

"What do you mean, 'We don't face any death angel?' Can you live forever?"

"No," replies Matt, "everyone dies sometime."

"Well," says Charlie, "God was teaching a spiritual truth through their physical experience. They faced coming death; so do we. And in that death, there was the judgment of God. We will face God's judgment, too. There was an escape from God's judgment in the blood of the lamb. Where is our escape? That's what we're going to read. Watch for the parallels between what we've read and its fulfillment in Jesus."

(Please catch these points: We, too, face death; we face God's judgment; and last, just as God provided an escape for them, he has for us.)

"Matt, why don't you read the story, and I'll follow in my Bible. Start with verse 17 and read down through 30. By the way, this was the celebration of Passover by Jesus and his men, just before he died."

Matt then reads the verses.

"OK," says Charlie, "look at verse 26. The bread that he took and broke is the aphikoman. What did he mean when he said, this is my body?"

"Beats me," replies Matt.

"What's the meaning of having bread without leaven?"

"Removing the chametz—the leaven—represents removing the sin from our lives."

"Has anyone ever removed **everything** wrong, **everything** that was disobedient to God, **every** potential of breaking the Law?" asks Charlie.

"No."

"Well, Jesus is claiming to be 'unleavened,' without sin—and claiming to be bread, their sustenance of life. But that's not all, he's saying that he is the fulfillment of all that the matzah represents in the Passover. In other words, he is claiming to be the reality that Passover teaches.

Matt, look at verse 27 and 28. He says, 'This is my blood of the covenant, which is poured out for the forgiveness of sins. What was he teaching them?"

"He says his blood can forgive sins, but I don't get the connection."

"It's this. He is saying that his blood can give protection from God's judgment for us, just like the Passover lamb's blood protected Israel."

Charlie then moves on to summarize the events of the arrest and trial of Messiah, and comes back to the scripture for the story of Jesus' death.

"Matt, when Jesus and his men ate the Passover, he told them that he was the reality that the Passover represented. Do you see that this was his claim?"

"Yes. But Charlie, there was no death angel that night. No one died, except him."

"That's true, but he was claiming to be their protection from God's eternal judgment. He was promising them—and us—eternal life, not physical life. Do you see that?"

"Yes."

"Well, Matt, the critical question is, can he do it? How can we know whether he can beat death for you and me? He needs to prove it, by beating death for himself. Look at the rest of the story."

Charlie then reads the text telling of the resurrection of Jesus and turns again to Matt.

"Matt, if Jesus wasn't raised, why didn't the Jewish religious leaders go get his body and show everyone he was dead? Why didn't the Romans? The best answer is that they couldn't, because the record is true."

At this point, there will always be several "what ifs." They will be the standard ones, such as, "What if the disciples came back, took the body, and lied about the resurrection?" If that "what if" is asked, go back and read Peter's denials and then ask what would make him brave enough to lead an attack of the guards for the body? Review the fact that the details of the Messiah's life were foretold, including how he would die and yet live forever. Challenge the idea that such a complex set of circumstances was in the control of the disciples.

The attempts to explain the absence of the body are not new and they are not unique to Jewish skeptics. Use the same answers to these objections as you use when others raise them. If you need help in this area, the book, *Evidence that Demands a Verdict*, by Josh McDowell is a good source.

If your "Matt" accepts Jesus as his Savior because you, like John the Baptist, have said, "Behold the (Passover) Lamb of God"—praise God! However, at this stage the major goal is to move Jesus from being an irrelevant Gentile god to being worth considering. When you reach this point, study of the Messianic prophecies comes into play. That is the subject of the next chapter.

Chapter 20
PROPHECIES REQUIRING A DECISION

GOAL No. 5

To show that Jesus is the Messiah and that we accept or reject him without any middle ground.

Most limit Jewish evangelism to sharing Messianic prophecies fulfilled by Jesus. Often this is ineffective—not because the prophecies lack power, but because of our timing and selection. If so, when is the time to suggest a serious study of Messianic prophecies? Which are the best to use? The simple answer—and the right answer—is to share when the Holy Spirit tells you to do so and to share the ones he suggests.

MAP CHECK!

No. 1: Our God is a PERSONAL God

No. 2: The BIBLE is God's Self-Revelation to us

No. 3: Salvation only comes God's Way, by BLOOD

Let's review the process that should have preceded this point. First, one must realize that God is interested in him. By now, he must neither think of God as a disinterested creator, nor as a detached force. We should have brought our friend to view God as (1) our Creator, (2) who is caring, and (3) communicative.

Second, our friend must have come to the point of accepting the Bible as the record of God's self-revelation and the basis for truth. If we later base our efforts on the authority of the scripture, we must first establish that it has a special authority above human brilliance.

Third, to move toward God, we must see that we need him. Our major needs are atonement and redemption—Yom Kippur and Pesach. Until our Jewish friend—or our Gentile friend for that matter—sees God as interested in him, and feels he needs God's help, there will be no interest in Jesus or any other mediator.

When then do you get into the Messianic prophecies? The right time is when your friend recognizes his need for a redeemer who atones. When he recognizes his need and is willing to trust the Bible as an authority to guide his decisions, you then share

God's answer. You look in the Hebrew scriptures at the salvation role of the Messiah and what his identifying marks will be. Then you go to the record in the Greek scriptures and basically say, "Here he is!"

The mechanics of sharing these prophecies can follow one of two ways. If your friend has gained some knowledge of the gospel—either through what you have shared, reading the New Testament, or through some other witness—then it is time to go directly through the Messianic prophecies. In most cases, though, it will be more profitable to deal with them as a part of a Bible study of Matthew.

Become familiar with the prophecies before you share them with others. It is also wise to stay with those whose fulfillment is more obvious. Seeing Jesus in some of the prophecies only develops with a Biblical background that your friend will not yet have. Therefore, stay away from the shadows and types and stick to the direct prophecies.

For example, Micah 5:2-5 is clear. It obviously promises a coming king, to be born in Bethlehem, who is someone more than a mere human. On the other hand, Psalm 41:9, read in context, is not so obvious. It says, "Even my close friend, whom I trusted, he who shared my bread, has lifted up his heel against me." Many see the betrayal by Judas foretold here, though it is David's lament. Saying this foretells the betrayal of Jesus may be true, but using it as a proof-text is more apt to create skepticism than faith.

After you have picked which prophecies you feel will be the most effective, you face another question. Which should you do—take them in the order of the books of the Bible or the order of their fulfillment? For example, if you take them book by book, you don't have to turn from source to source. The problem is that they don't fall in a chronology of Jesus' life. On the other hand, if you start with the prophecies of Jesus' birth and move to those of his death, you skip all over the Hebrew scriptures, which is hard for a beginning Bible student. Either way, write down what you conclude with each prophecy. It is even better if you can get your friend to make the notes.

Write down what each prophecy foretells collecting the conclusions into a final composite. Otherwise the individual verses will continue to swirl around in his head and not settle into a total picture. If so, he will elect to decide later when he is less confused. Remember, confusion is a major tactic of Satan. Be alert to minimize it!

If you are doing a Bible study, such as Matthew, then you will deal with the prophecies as they are fulfilled in the gospel. In fact, Matthew helps you by quoting the major ones. Again, unless your friend is familiar with the gospel, this is generally the better strategy. It will take a greater time commitment on your part, but remember what Paul said "...the **gospel** is the power unto salvation...." Scripture always carries more power than our commentary on it.

Your time of common Bible study may have been his first exposure and now the Holy Spirit is drawing him to consider the validity of what he has read. In this case, the Hebrew scriptures foretelling Jesus provides the validity of the New Testament record.

Again, remember it is critical to avoid two things: confusion and loss of credibility. Confusion always gives an opportunity to delay decisions. The basis for conclusions found in today's logic crumble with time because the facts are forgotten. Promises to "think about it" are rarely kept. People forget confusing things as quickly as they can, rather than trying to untangle them.

The other point deals with our need of credibility when we are asking a person to accept our views. People fear making a mistake. When we are sure of something and they are not, they fear that we may have been fooled into believing something that isn't valid. After all, if something is true, most feel it should be obvious to everyone—especially them. Now they face the risk that we may convince them of our misconception. They certainly don't want to be fooled by someone who has been fooled!

What then does this apprehension have to do with our image of credibility? It's simple. If our friend doesn't see the application to Jesus in the prophecies we use, he will either think we have been fooled or are trying to fool him. He is already suspicious; we must not give him support for that skepticism. A few irrefutable prophecies are worth more than a hundred types and shadows. Stay with the clear texts!

A time where the two of you set down with pencil and paper, two Bibles, a concordance, Bible dictionary, and a wall full of commentary on the Hebrew and Greek will be the exception. That setting rarely exists and if it does, will not be until several sorties have tested your credibility. Most of these opportunities will be at times when you have nothing with you except what is in your head. It will be a passing question or an opportunity brought by the conversation. You need to respond with strong prophecies, quoted from memory. Be prepared! You can offer to get back with the answer later, but too often, when the moment passes, it is gone.

What leaves Jewish people incredulous is the Christian claim that Jesus was both God and man. You may have an explanation for that paradox that satisfies you, but there is no guarantee that it will satisfy your friend. Don't use it—at least not initially; he may fail to see your logic. Once the Bible has been accepted as the Word of God, make the Bible—not human logic—the primary authority for judging truth. Begin with the scripture that says the Messiah will be both God and man, whether anyone ever understands it or not. Take your stand on the prophecy, not on your ability to explain the physics.

Because of the Jewish stress that God is nothing like a man and the seeming logic that if something is white it can't be black, Isaiah 9:6 is the Bible's most important Messianic verse. **Memorize it** and grasp what the words say! "For unto us a child is born, unto us a son is given, and the government shall rest on his shoulders and his name shall be called Wonderful Counselor, Mighty God, Everlasting Father, Prince of Peace."

This clearly declares that this great future king, the Messiah, will be both human and divine. This king will be born as a Jewish—human—child. Isaiah refers to his people when he says this child will be born "unto us." Being born "unto us" and called a son certainly makes this person human. When you get to the names which describe him, however, he is obviously a human child that is God himself. No Hebrew prophet would have described a mere human as "El Gibbor" which we translate "Mighty God." This identical term is used by Jeremiah when he says, "The great, the mighty God (El Gibbor)—Jehovah is his name."[26]

Though you may need to bring it up, rather than being asked, the second most important scripture is Daniel 9:25. The point of this scripture is that if Jesus wasn't the Messiah, **everyone** has missed him. His time to come ran out almost 2,000 years ago!

You will need to know some history to support your point. In Daniel 9:25, we read "From the issuing of the decree to restore and rebuild Jerusalem until the **Messiah**, the ruler, comes, there will be 'seven sevens,' and '62 sevens.' Most translate Messiah in this passage as "the Anointed One," which is what Messiah literally

---

[26] Jeremiah 32:18, NIV.

means; still, if your friend looks it up in his Hebrew Bible, he will find that it is literally "Messiah."

This verse says that Messiah is coming 483 years (7x7 + 62x7) after the decree to rebuilt Jerusalem. Cyrus of Persia gave that decree in 536 B.C. The point is that if Daniel is telling us the truth, Messiah is not coming somewhere out in the fuzzy future as Rabbinic Judaism holds. If Daniel is right, he has already come.

If your friend is the least bit alert, he will see that this doesn't fit the time of Jesus either! What is the explanation, then? Various scholars have strained to make all sorts of combinations of time fit these dates. Their mistake is trying to adjust Daniel rather than the calendar. Our dating of events in ancient history is based on the Ptolemaic calendar, which is incomplete between Daniel and Jesus. The holes have been filled in by guess work. In fact, it seems to be off 82 years![27]

The point is not to prove that Jesus was born on December 25, 0 A.D. Avoid that trap! We don't know the month, day, or year of his birth. He was most likely born about 5 B.C. (**Remember**, Christian tradition set his birth date, not the Bible. Never try to defend Christian tradition or you will be embarrassed. The scripture is our authority, not church policies through the ages.) Also, just as those who formed the Ptolemaic calendar guessed at the lost years, so too, Christians have to guess at its length. Thus, you can't prove that Jesus came exactly 483 years after Cyrus' decree—though it is a very safe assumption. What you **can prove** is that if Jesus wasn't the Messiah, everyone missed him and he has already come. This prophecy gives a window of time in which to search for the Messiah. No one else in this time frame—or since, for that matter—even came close.

---

[27] Martin Anstey, *Chronology of the Old Testament* (Grand Rapids, Michigan: Kregel Publications, 1973), pp 9-16.

Another potential question you need to prepare to face is the claim that Jesus couldn't have been the Messiah because the world is still not at peace. If you are asked this question, the probability is that you have stirred up questions in your friend that he has asked his rabbi. Now armed with a "stumper" he is back to challenge you and Christianity.

The question, "Why is the world not at peace if Jesus is the Messiah?" is best answered with another question. (Replying to a question with a question is a good Jewish tactic.) Jesus did this when the Jewish leaders asked him what right he had to teach in the temple. He basically said, "Answer this and I'll tell you, was John the Baptist of God or man?" Your response is, "Answer this and I'll tell you, why do some rabbis say there will be a Messiah ben David and a Messiah ben Joseph?"

With rare exception he won't have the foggiest notion that Rabbinic thought deals with two Messiahs. Whether he knows the reason or not, your response should be that while Rabbinic Judaism expects two messiahs coming at different times, the Bible calls for **one** Messiah who comes **twice**. Peace will come when he returns as ruler.

Once the explanation is given as to when peace will come, take the initiative. Stress why the Messiah needed to come the first time—as a sacrifice for sins, fulfilling Yom Kippur, Pesach, and so on. After that, pose the question, "How will you face his rule when he returns, unless you deal with what he did for you when he first came?"

When the time to set down and go through the Messianic scriptures finally arrives, you should be prepared to ask for a decision if your friend agrees that Jesus fulfilled them. In sales terms, study of the Messianic prophecies brings us to the "close." Save it until you have a prospect that is "ready to buy, if the claims of the product hold up."

Explain that God—a bit at a time down through the history of Israel—revealed his plan for redeeming mankind. Then deal with the scriptures that are given as Israel's history develops. What though about the confusion as to when they were fulfilled? Hopefully, by this time, your Jewish friend will be aware of the gospel, but don't depend on his knowledge being adequate.

Before you start, make a list of the scriptures you plan to share. Make a second copy for your friend so he can study on his own if he wants. When you start the study, take a piece of paper and divide the page with the following headings:

Origins: human and divine
Birth: where, when, and how
Ministry: prophet, priest, and king
Redemption: Death, burial, and resurrection
How does this effect me?

This should give you three or four lines between each heading. (Or you can put each heading at the top of an individual page.) Then as you go through the Hebrew scriptures and pick up prophecies, list them under the heading they foretell. Though handwritten, your entries should be something like this:

Birth: where, when, and how

Isa. 7:13,14	*Born of a virgin*
Dan. 9:24-27	*Exact time of birth*
Micah 5:2-5	*To be born in Bethlehem*

When you finish, this should give a picture of the Messiah Israel should have expected. Then go through the gospels and show where Jesus fulfilled each.

A word of caution: watch your time. It is better to approach this as a multi-session Bible study than to try to cover everything in one meeting. A good rule of thumb is to limit your conversation. Forty-five minutes to an hour should be the maximum session length, unless your friend insists on continuing. Anything longer brings diminishing returns. Again, if you jointly list your conclusions as you go through each prophecy, you can review them the next session and continue.

The Appendix includes a list of Messianic prophecies, some background material for each, and the reference for their fulfillment. However, remember Jesus admonition to us: "Be wise as serpents and as innocent as doves." It is wiser to write out whatever you plan to use than to photocopy it from the book. If you are lazy and bring photocopied pages to the study, your friend is apt to ask about your source. Books on evangelism frighten unsaved people and your Jewish friend will be no exception.

After you study the Old Testament passages and list the conclusions from each, look up the fulfillment. Write the reference at the right of the page as shown below:

Birth: where, when, and how

Isa. 7:13,14	*Born of a virgin*	*Luke 1:26-38*
Dan. 9:24-27	*Exact time of birth*	*Luke 2: 1-3*
Micah 5:2-5	*To be born in Bethlehem*	*Luke 2: 4-7*

As you study the passages and make your notes, only write the meaning that you both come to agree the passage says. If you run into disagreement, work on the meaning of the passage until you agree. If you can't agree, scratch that one and don't list it.

You need to write down only the opinions about which you agree. This prevents holes in his expectancy of the Messiah without you knowing it. When the picture begins to form, it needs to be made up of parts that he accepts. Otherwise, he may say, "Well, that may prove it to you, but it doesn't prove it to me." However, if the proof of Jesus' Messiahship is built on his understanding of the prophecies, he can't do that. You can coach him and help him understand the passages, but get their meaning worked out before you begin to look up their fulfillment in the gospels.

Chapter 21
ASKING FOR A DECISION

In evangelism, as in every other endeavor that involves persuasion, there comes a time when we must ask for a decision in favor of what we argue to be true. In sales, this is called the "close." Every salesman, evangelist, and just plain average person, would like to avoid facing it if there were any alternative; but there isn't.

It is the nature of people to avoid every decision they can. If we could avoid all decisions, we would make no mistakes—and avoiding mistakes is a major goal of life! Worse yet, the more critical the decision, the more we attempt to avoid it. Heaven and Hell are about as critical as decisions come; thus, it shouldn't surprise us that people attempt to put off such an awesome chance for error.

The problem is that a lack of decision for Jesus leaves one damned. We can't allow others the comfort of avoiding that choice. More to the point, they are not the only ones who feel the pressure of that moment. When we call for a commitment to Jesus, we step under that emotional weight with them. It is as risky to require a decision as to be asked for one. Thus, most Christians "chicken-out" when it is time to ask for a decision.

Many see pressing for a decision as presumptuous. Those who feel that way are naive about human nature and the nature of the spiritual realm. While the Holy

Spirit is calling a person to decide for Jesus, Satan is giving him every possible reason to put it off. Satan knows that a decision delayed is a decision against Jesus.

Anyone who believes that we make our decision for Jesus in a neutral spiritual environment is Biblically shallow. Thus, from a spiritual perspective, our persuasion—or really God's call through us—is needed to offset Satanic influence to procrastinate.

On the purely human plane, people are insecure in their decisions and need encouragement that they are right. If we don't try to strongly convince our friend that Jesus is the way, the truth, and the life, we give him no support in a very difficult time.

The point is, at some time, you must require your friend to decide for or against Jesus as his way to God. Not challenging him to decide—for or against—is cowardly and unkind.

But what if he says no to you and Jesus; what have you lost? Is he any less damned than before you asked? The only risk to us is a minor challenge to our convictions. More importantly, the risk is negligible if we really love the person. Remember, "love covers a multitude of sins," including making friends uncomfortable by requiring them to face an important decision in their lives.

Ultimately, evidence calls for a commitment. We are not involved in an academic curiosity. Non-Jewish Christians, however, need to be understanding of the added tension at this point in the lives of their Jewish friends. They face the added pressure of being counted as traitors to their people if they accept Jesus. This runs so deeply that some would rather miss salvation than suffer the opposition of their family. The fact that your Jewish friend eventually believes that Jesus is the Messiah does not guarantee he will choose Jesus over his people.

Only the Holy Spirit can handle this problem. We can help, but it's out of our hands. Hopefully, there will have been earlier opportunities to explain that being Jewish is ethnic, not religious. This is a time to remind a Jewish person that accepting the Jewish Messiah makes him true to his heritage, not a traitor.

The cost of accepting Jesus that the Jewish seeker faces is rejection by his family and his people. The degree will vary from disapproval to cutting off all contact. We need to be sensitive to this and not minimize it. We need to agree that we know this may happen, but that God will be his family if other family members abandon him.

We can strengthen the promise that accepting Jesus will not cut the Jewish person off from his roots by letting him know of Jewish believers. If you know Jewish believers, introduce him to them early in the process.

You can share that the church was totally Jewish for its first 15 years and that Jewish Christians have existed ever since. No one knows the current number of Jewish believers, but it is significant and growing. As early as 1972, when the current surge of Jewish believers first gained notice, *Time* magazine (June 12, 1972, pp. 66-67) reported that U.C.L.A. campus rabbi, Rabbi Shlomo Cunin, estimated that 6,000 to 7,000 a year were accepting Jesus. Don't minimize the cost of accepting Jesus, but guarantee your friend that it is worth it. Assure him that he will not be alone in the Jewish community.

What do you do then, when it is time to ask for a commitment? At this stage, do basically what you would do if you were talking to a non-Jewish person.

No matter what the ethnic background, we should always try to answer objections before we ask our friend to give his life to Jesus. If we ask him to decide while there is still confusion or fear he will try to postpone his decision and justify his delay.

Once someone begins to justify why he didn't chose what you suggested, he will continue to support that decision in order to save face. His mind shifts gears. He is no longer thinking about what you have said. Rather, he moves into a defensive posture and concentrates on how to win the mental tug of war. Your logic about why Jesus is the Messiah, or how he fulfilled the prophecies becomes neutralized because Jesus is no longer the question. It is now defending his position.

Charlie has reached the day to call for a decision from Matt. Let's listen.

"Matt, we've talked a lot over the last year about God and I've enjoyed it."

"Me, too, Charlie."

"Do you think you could identify the Messiah from prophecy?"

Matt pauses for some time before he replies. Finally he says, "Yes."

"Matt, how good do we have to be—to be with God?" asks Charlie.

"Well, if you do the best you can, what more can God require of you?" responds Matt.

"Listen, Matt," says Charlie, "first of all, nobody **does** the best he can. We only approach our best on those rare times when we are under extreme pressure. Most of our life is spent, sliding by without putting out much effort. When you die, do you really want to be judged on the basis of whether you have always done your best?"

"I don't know, Charlie, I haven't been a bad person, I haven't killed anybody."

"Well, that's not good enough! God tells us in his word that everything in his presence is perfect—which means that everyone there will have to be perfect. Do you think God is going to lower heaven's perfection to the best humanity can do? If he did, it would be the same mess as this world. If that's heaven, who needs it?

"Nobody's perfect, Charlie."

"Right! That means that unless we can perfect ourselves—or someone else makes us perfect, we have no hope. You can't perfect yourself, or you would have already done it—right?

Matt, we have another problem. Even on your nicest day—do you think you can beat death?"

"No."

"If you can't jump up to heaven, now—while you are strong and healthy, how do you expect to, when you are weak and dying? Just being a good person doesn't solve our problem.

Solomon tells us in Proverbs 14:10, 'There is a way that seems right to man, but in the end it leads to death.' No matter what we do—exercise, take vitamins, breath clean air, live morally, or whatever—we die!

If we get to heaven, someone with supernatural power has to come and take us there. Would you agree?"

"I don't know—I just hope God will take care of me somehow, I guess."

"Well, Matt, God has taken care of us. Think a minute—why wasn't anyone exempt from Yom Kippur or Pesach?"

"I don't know, Charlie, why?"

"In the Bible, no one was exempt, because everyone needs the mercy of atonement. God's justice requires the penalty of sin to be paid—but his mercy allows a substitute. That's the meaning of Yom Kippur.

Do you remember the two goats? Entry into God's presence came by one's death; the other carried the sins away. If anyone had been 'good enough,' to not need atonement, they would have been exempt from Yom Kippur. No one was!

Passover was God's judgment through the death angel. However, those protected by the lamb's blood escaped judgment.

On Yom Kippur, Israel came before God by God's grace. And that grace was through the blood of a substitute. On Pesach, the blood of the Passover lamb protected them from judgment. Leviticus 17:11 says, '...it is the blood that makes atonement for one's life.' Do you know of any other way?"

"No, Charlie, but what's that got to do with us?"

"Today, where do we turn for a sacrificial substitute, acceptable to God?"

"I don't know."

"Prophecy tells us the Messiah will be God's sacrificial lamb for all men. In a vision of the Messiah, Isaiah 53:6 records the following: 'All we, like sheep, have gone astray. Each of us has turned to his own way. And Jehovah has laid on him'—the Messiah—'the iniquity of us all.' Do you understand that being our acceptable substitute is part of the Messiah's role?"

"Yes."

"Matt, many prophecies talk about the Messiah being a prophet and king. Speaking of the Messiah, Moses says in Deuteronomy 18:15, 'Jehovah, your God, will raise up a prophet like me from among your own brothers. You **must** listen to him.' If the Messiah speaks for God—and is, himself, the king—then we should obey him above all others. **Would you agree?**"

"Yes."

Charlie hopes Matt can't hear his heart beat. He always gets nervous at this point. He tries to keep his voice steady and continues, "Matt, do you think that Jesus was the Messiah?"

"I'm not sure," says Matt.

"Well, let's look at the facts. When does Daniel say that the Messiah will come?"

"When Jesus came on the scene."

"That's right, Matt, in fact the three wise men in the Christmas story were probably Persian astronomers who knew about Daniel's prophecy."

Charlie continues, "Where was he to be born?"

"Bethlehem."

"Most important, Matt, what kind of person does prophecy say the Messiah will be?"

"Charlie, that's the hardest part. It says he will be both God and man, and I don't see how that could be."

"Matt, I don't think anyone can explain that, but could God become a man if he chose to?"

"Yes."

"Then the question is, "Did he do it? What about the resurrection? Do you think that's true?"

"If he were God and man, that's no problem."

"Do you think he was?"

Again, Matt waits an uncomfortably long time before he replies. Charlie is tense, too, but has learned to wait when someone is under conviction.
Eventually, Matt says, "Yes, I think he was. I believe he was the Messiah."

Trying to breathe smoothly and not show his nervousness, Charlie continues, "Matt, do you know the salvation promise Jesus made to you?"

"No," replies Matt.

"The Bible says, **For God so loved the world...** that's you and me, not the dirt... **that he gave his only begotten Son...** that's Jesus of Nazareth, who was God who came and became a man.... **that whosoever...** tall or short, good or bad... **believed in him would not perish...** that is, not spend eternity in Hell cut off from God... **but have everlasting life...** which is to live perfectly, forever.

Do you know what it means to believe in him? It isn't just believing Jesus was who he claimed to be. Satan knows that's so, and he isn't saved. To believe in him means to depend on him. It's like when you need a doctor. You go to one you 'believe in.' You put yourself in his hands and whether you live or die depends on him. God promises that when we put ourselves in the hands of Jesus—and depend on him in this same way—he will guarantee that we will not perish, but have everlasting life.

Yom Kippur was a picture of what God would appear to do for us. Jesus' blood allows our entry into God's presence and he also carried our sins away.

That our part of salvation is to trust should not surprise us. Do you remember why Adam was put out of the Garden? It was because he wanted to be independent of God's control. He wanted to trust himself, and his ability to judge what was good for him and what was evil for him—rather than trust God. If we got into trouble because we didn't want to depend on God, what would you think he would require for us to come home? The obvious answer is that we must choose to be dependent on God, rather than self. Do you think Jesus can give you eternal life, if you depend on him?"

After a few moments, Matt responds, "Yes."

"Matt, in a lot of places people are killed if they accept Jesus; but let me ask you—are they smart to gain eternal life, even if it costs them their physical life?"

"Sure."

"Matt, what about you? Are you willing to trust Jesus and follow him, even if it costs you?"

A long silence passes. Charlie feels his heart beating for what seems an eternity. He wants to jump back in the conversation and make a comment to relieve the tension, but he has learned the value of silence. He has asked for a commitment; now he must force himself to be silent until he gets a response, no matter how much time passes.

Eventually, Matt replies, "How do I do that, Charlie?"

SOME ADDITIONAL THOUGHTS

If you look at the conversation between Charlie and Matt, there are some notable absences. For example, no where is Matt asked to "convert" or to become a "Christian." Neither is there any discussion at this stage about being baptized.

In the Jewish mind, "to convert" means to change from loyalty to the Jewish people to allegiance to their persecutors. It does not mean a death of an "old nature" and a birth of a "new." Don't use the term, it will only get in your way. Second, the purpose of this conversation was to get Matt saved. The attempt to get him comfortable enough with institutional Christianity to join a church is a second and equally difficult battle. Charlie wisely didn't endanger the current cause by trying to fight on two fronts.

When your Jewish friend makes that commitment of faith, you must begin to solidify that decision with Biblical affirmation that his choice was right. Spiritually, he is a newborn babe, requiring maximum care and attention. How to give that spiritual pediatric care is a major part of the next chapter. Following that, we will look at ways to help him become comfortable enough with Christianity to consider becoming a part of a local church.

Chapter 22
THE SABBATH AND SUNDAY

GOAL No. 6

To lead the new Jewish believer through his initial spiritual growth and into the corporate nurture of a congregation.

Initial spiritual nurture is pivotal for every new believer, but it is critical if that newborn is Jewish. The shift from Shabbot to Sunday is difficult, even if he never attended synagogue.

Discipleship, or Christian nurture, is a fairly new subject in church life. Its elements were always there, but formal programs are a recent development. Why then has this need grown in recent years? Perhaps more correctly, why did the old informal system cease to work?

It is speculation, but the most probable cause for the need of more formal nurturing is the decrease of Christian influence in society. In the past, church was respected and viewed in a positive way. The non-churched held it in the same esteem as the "black-sheep of the family" held the home. He may not have wanted to live by its standards, but he still had a nostalgic place for it in his heart.

With that attitude, when someone got saved, they willingly—automatically—returned to church, already knowing its values, activities, and attitudes. In short, having grown up in a church culture, they just came home.

Today—at least in the pluralistic cities—most are not coming home when they visit church. They are visiting a foreign country with new and strange ways. Worse, if they are Jewish, they feel they are traveling in a hostile country, as well. Little wonder they don't "make themselves at home."

Whatever the reason, America's Jewish believers are basically unchurched. We have little or no data by which to judge how many are in congregations. However, the little that exists suggests only two to four percent ever get involved in congregational life. That means that about 95 percent live their Christian lives, alone, undeveloped, and unproductive.

New Jewish believers have the same developmental needs as any other spiritual newborn, plus some added ones. For example, spiritual growth follows the same pattern as physical birth and growth. When a child is physically born, it needs a great deal of care and guidance. For the first few days, this is almost totally provided by its mother. So too, for the spiritual newborn, the evangelist (the one God used to reach them) occupies a similar role. No one else enjoys the same trust level from the new Christian.

This is why individual discipleship of the new believer is so critical. Expecting the church to provide the needed teaching and nurture is like expecting a physical newborn to show up in the kitchen for regular meals. Both need a time of special feeding to survive.

Where then do you get the spiritual babyfood you need for your Christian newborn? The first place to check is your church. If it has good nurturing material for new believers, use it. Again, a note of caution: if your church's program is limited to group activities, such as a "newcomers class," don't substitute classes for personal attention. In the first week following salvation, you need to check on your friend often, not have someone else do it on Sunday—if he, or she, happens to come to church. Such a class is good, but the new believer—especially if he is Jewish—will initially need much more personal attention. If you don't find what you need at church, check the nearest Christian book store.

Perhaps the best known material comes from Campus Crusade and from the Navigators. Jews for Jesus and other Jewish mission groups publish material for new believers who are Jewish. (See note below if you need their addresses.)[28]

Personal one-on-one nurture should begin immediately. Thus, you should have the material before you need it. Whatever plan you follow, you will find some common elements. For example, the initial study should be the scriptural basis for salvation. This confirms the validity of the recent decision on the basis of scripture. Satan's attack of the new Christian often brings a feeling of "What have I done? Did I make a mistake? Am I really saved?" You can minimize this and its destructive power by anchoring the plan of salvation in his or her mind with this first Bible study.

---

[28] If needed, their mailing addresses are:

Campus Crusade for Christ, 7094 Newbury Avenue, San Bernardino CA 92404

Jews for Jesus, 60 Haight Street, San Francisco CA 94102

NavPress, Box 6000, Colorado Springs CO 80934

You should get your newborn into prayer immediately. Also, take him or her to church with you at the very first service possible. Don't expect him to be any more prone to meet you there, than you would expect a child to meet you at school on his first school day. **Take him**! Don't just invite him to come!

While you are in church, explain everything that happens. Don't assume he will know what comes next, when to stand, or what a hymnal is; he won't. Save him some embarrassment by explaining things before he has to ask. Remember if you were attending a synagogue for the first time, you would appreciate the help.

The four common elements of all nurturing material are Bible study, prayer, church attendance, and witnessing. Generally the new believer is asked to tell those close to him—his family or friends—that he has trusted Jesus. When the new believer is Jewish, the telling of that decision—especially to family and friends—should be approached with caution. He or she needs to share that decision in every situation that will strengthen that new spiritual life. Sharing it, naively, with his or her Jewish family, can be destructive to both. Preparation on how to share that decision should precede the announcement.

For those from a church background, witnessing is immediately encouraged. When they share that they have trusted Jesus, they get a positive affirmation and their faith is strengthened. That is not the case for one from a Jewish, Islamic, Hindu, or secular ancestry. Thus, they need time for their faith to grow a bit, and time to be equipped for the assault that this information will bring.

Again, as with physical growth, there comes a time for the spiritual "child" to expand his exposure in the Kingdom. Just as a child expands his source of nurture from mother to immediate kin, and eventually into the society around him, so too, the spiritual child needs to begin to be nurtured by others in addition to the initial evangelist. In short, he needs congregational nurture to develop fully.

The parallel of the physical family is the Christian small group. For most churches, this is an adult Bible class. It may be part of Sunday School or a home group, but it needs to be small enough for everyone to know each other. Don't try to get a commitment to join the church until he is comfortable and feels a part of a smaller unit. Let him develop some social ties and grow in the Lord first.

The congregational worship gathering parallels a child's neighborhood. Eventually he has to deal with the larger world, the Church consisting of believers who differ from him and his "family."

Each of these levels of expanded acceptance of other Christians requires growth. The initial problem is getting him "out of the house to go to school"—that is, replacing the evangelist with the congregation as his spiritual teacher. Part of the problem is that everyone acts out of habit and assumes the rest of the world does exactly as he does. Thus, the new Jewish believer will assume that church now fills the same role as synagogue once filled.

For most, the synagogue was somewhere they went once a year for a very special religious occasion. Also, it was more of a Jewish community center than a place to meet God. For one thing, your friend may not be too sure he wants to be involved in the "Christian" community. (He may still think in old ways of Christian being anti-Jewish.) Second, if he didn't attend synagogue before, why should he attend church now? The point is that you will need to show him the value of a weekly corporate worship, or he will assume it is unnecessary.

Though you may not be able to affect it, your church needs to offer something of value or he won't come. He won't attend out of "oughtness" or nostalgia, like some who grew up in church. If the program doesn't meet his needs, he will shortly—at best—change churches. At worse, he will stop going anywhere.

All of the problems in getting the new Jewish believer into church isn't with the "spiritual child." You may have to do some educating of friends about Jewish sensitivities. You may have to enlighten them that "Jew-jokes" are not acceptable. In some cases, you may have to be like Paul when he rebuked Peter, and stand against racist attitudes in your church. Whatever you have to do, you must be the protective "big brother or sister," until your friend no longer feels like the "new kid at school."

Chapter 23
HOW TO TELL THE FAMILY

The natural tendency of everyone who finds a new truth—especially one that is life changing—is to want to tell others. This seems to be intensified with Jewish believers because they realize that their relatives and Jewish friends have never been told. It is also so clear to them that they can't understand why it won't be clear to their family—if they can just explain it to them.

Sadly, the family rarely reacts that way. With few exceptions, acceptance of Jesus as Messiah is greeted with hostility and seen as a betrayal of the Jewish people. At this point, the common plea is, "Give your own religion a chance." This focuses on the claim that your friend wouldn't have done this if he had known enough about Rabbinic Judaism. The natural request that follows is that, "out of fairness to his lineage, he learn more about Judaism before he converts." That request can range from being asked to visit a rabbi to being kidnapped for deprogramming. No matter what the level of pressure to abandon his trust in Jesus, the new believer should not be exposed to it before he has the basics under his belt.

In fact, you should forewarn your friend that his family may ask him for promises that he must not give. They may ask him to promise not to go to church, or never to witness. The easiest—and least threatening response—is to say its to soon to make any promises about what he will do. (If you don't make unwise promises, you don't have to worry about how to get out of them!)

One very likely request will be to talk to a rabbi. Recommend that the new believer decline, if possible. The goal of the family and the rabbi is to convince the new believer to give up his or her faith. By agreeing to meet with the rabbi, he or she is telling the family, "It's okay for you to not respect my personal decision."

Loving parents, on occasion, do not respect the personal decisions of their children. If the family insists, then suggest the new believer promise to go six months later, after he knows enough about Christianity to ask the rabbi intelligent questions. If this is phrased right, those who love him should accept it as fair and give him time to grow in faith and knowledge. If your friend can't resist the family pressure and follow this advice, he or she should insist on choosing the rabbi and going alone. Individual discussions with a rabbi are, with rare exception, civil. Group meetings are emotional and often messy.

How and when do you suggest that your friend tell his family? Along with the things to do, there are some things not to do! One of the most important principles is not to make this a public pronouncement! Remind him that people—even those of his home—need to be able to save face. Have him tell his relatives, one at a time, privately, beginning with the one he expects to be the most sympathetic. If family members are open to the truth he has found, telling them privately relieves them of the group pressure to reject it.

Perhaps the second most important principle is to share the decision in a casual non-confronting way. He must remember that the first step in persuasion is to get the other party to accept that it is within reason for him to hold the disputed view. So too, members of the Jewish believer's family need to have time to accept his being a Christian, before they are asked to join him!

Until they accept that the decision was acceptable **for him**, forceful proclamation will be a mistake.

Suggest that the new Jewish believer not have a rehearsed speech. Those of the Jewish community will be hard to convince that he wasn't rehearsed by some missionary. Rather, suggest trusting the Holy Spirit to give him what he needs to say. Whatever is said must carry a second message; that is, that he still loves the family and is as committed to them and the Jewish people as ever.

Last, but certainly not least, remind your friend that God does the persuasion in human hearts, but that our prayers affect that outcome. Remind him—and yourself—that prayer is more effective in changing hearts than we are prone to believe.

The sharing of his witness is still a necessary part of his nurture. The only caution is when and how. As for the way to do it, he must bring his family and friends through the same steps he walked. Just as he has believed, individuals of his house will also have to come to believe that:

1) there is a Creator God who is personal, who therefore cares and communicates through the scriptures;

2) that, according to the scriptures, man's redemption has always been by blood and blood only;

3) that, according to the scriptures, the Messiah would be the God-man who would come as the Lamb of God;

4) and that Jesus is the Messiah!

Appendix
COMMENTARY ON
KEY SCRIPTURE VERSES

VERSE INDEX

GENESIS COMMENTARY

If you develop a study of Genesis, be alert for the unfolding of God's redemptive plan. Look for the development of the covenant relationship between God and man. The most basic form of that covenant is, "I will be your God and you will be my people." Though this is not directly stated, it is an understood truth in the very act of man's creation.

Genesis also shows the beginnings of the struggle between God's truth and Satan's lie over the way of reconciliation, that is, whether it comes by God's grace or man's works.

Be careful of attempts to accommodate evolution by saying God directed a process, rather than creating directly. The danger is that this separates God from any direct involvement in our world. (Most of these attempts to accommodate the two misrepresent both the Bible and the theory of evolution.)

GOD AS CREATOR
Genesis 1:1-2

In the beginning God created the heavens and the earth. Now the earth was formless and empty, darkness was over the surface of the deep, and the Spirit of God was hovering over the waters.

Genesis 1:1 is a statement of fact that covers the universe. It credits Elohim (God of all power) as creating all that exists out of nothing. The Hebrew word, bara, which we translate "created," means to effect a special new entity. It is **not** just the rearrangement of existing energy and matter.

"In the beginning (creation of time) God created the heavens and the earth (space and matter)." Thus, the time-space-matter compendium[1] of the world's physics came into being.

Genesis 1:2 gives us the first element of creation; vast complexity, perfectly in order. Creation is scientifically far more defensible than the theory of evolution at this point. Evolution requires an exemption from the scientific law that—without outside intervention—complexity and order **always** decay into disorder and chaos. God energized this into being. (The Spirit of God "hovered" or "vibrated.")

Some claim there is a gap between verse one and two. They believe a catastrophe befell creation in that time through the revolt of Satan. Others have used this "gap" to try to reconcile the geological claims of vast time with Genesis. This attempt to reconcile the Bible to geology fails because the geological tables (unreliable as the fossil record is) would place death before the creation of man and his sin.

MAN, A MODEL OF GOD
Genesis 1:26-27

Then God said, "Let us make man in our image, in our likeness, and let them rule over the fish of the sea and the birds of the air, over the live-stock, over all the earth, and over all the creatures that move along the ground." So God created man in his own image, in the image of God he created him; male and female he created them.

On the sixth day, God makes the last unique creation ("bara.") This will be a creation with vast freedom. It will eventually be able to move in the sea, the air,and on land. More importantly, it is made to bridge the gap between the spiritual and physical worlds. It is Adam. He is like the animal—a soul creature, yet, inbreathed with the spirit of life. (Breath, wind, and spirit are all the same word in Hebrew.)

Here we have the basis of covenant relationship. In later self-revelation, God directly states that what that relationship was always meant to be: "I will be your God and you will be my people."

THIS CREATION, COMPLETED
Genesis 2:2-3

By the seventh day God had finished the work he had been doing; so on the seventh day he rested from all his work. And God blessed the seventh day and made it holy, because on it he rested from all the work of creating that he had done.

Thus, the creation of the universe was complete and God ceased from his work. He ceased from "bara"—creating new things.

God then "blessed" (the word means to gave special concern and interest) the seventh day because it signified the completion of this current universe and its physics.

Contrary to the theory of evolution, the Bible claims that creation was instantaneous (within the specific day,) and with the appearance of history. Plants and animals came into existence, mature and with the appearance of age. For example, if you had cut down a tree, it would have contained "annual rings," and would have appeared to be years old at its creation. So too, the light from the stars, created on the forth day, originated "in route" giving a superficial appearance of age.

"ECHAD," A CRITICAL WORD
Genesis 2:24

For this reason a man will leave his father and mother and be united to his wife, and they will become ***one*** *(echad) flesh.*

At this point we have a word used which will be important to understand in expressing God as Father, Son, and Spirit. In Genesis 2:24, Adam and Eve are said to become "one flesh." The word for one is "echad" (as in the Shema.) Its meaning (in both uses) is a compound unity, not an isolated uniqueness.

THE FALL
Genesis 3:1-5

Now the serpent was more crafty than any of the wild animals the LORD God had made. He said to the woman, "Did God really say, 'You must not eat from any tree in the garden?"

The woman said to the serpent, "We may eat fruit from the trees in the garden, but God did say, 'You must not eat fruit from the tree that is in the middle of the garden, and you must not touch it, or you will die."

"You will not surely die," the serpent said to the woman. For God knows that when you eat of it your eyes will be opened, and you will be like God, knowing good and evil."

Was the tree of the knowledge of good and evil placed in the garden to tempt man, or was it necessarily there, but dangerous? We believe the latter.

Two trees were there: the tree of the knowledge of good and evil and the tree of life. One gave life; the other cut man off from that life source.

The tree of life sustained life, reminding Adam with each bite that he was totally **dependent** upon God for life itself. The tree of the knowledge of good and evil offered **independence.** It would give one the ability to judge what was "good" for him, and what was "evil." This offered to produce the capacity of **independent judgment.** Therein lies the key to understanding its temptation. It was that one could "be god"—that is, each could be their own source of judgment as to their course of action.

Only God is independent, able to create without the aid of another, under no authority from above, exercising all authority over those below. This is still mankind's problem: it is wanting to exercise authority without being subject to it.

To love God, man had to be free to choose whether he would trust God (represented in the tree of life) or himself (represented by the tree of knowledge.) To make that choice, the opportunity to be self-guiding had to be available, even though it brought death. Despite warning, man's choice was self-rule which cut him off from the source of viability.

Man is free to choose God or self as his object of worship. Many will ask you, "Why didn't God make us so we couldn't sin?" The answer is that human beings are made to love God, and that love requires free choice. To be able to choose to love God, God had to let us **choose.** By definition, the ability to reject God and choose self as our God has to exist, or we are not free to choose God.

GOD'S INITIAL HINT OF FUTURE REDEMPTION
Genesis 3:13-15

Then the LORD God said to the woman, "What is this you have done?"

The woman said, "The serpent deceived me, and I ate."

So the LORD God said to the serpent, "Because you have done this, "Cursed are you above all the livestock and all the wild animals! You will crawl on your belly and you will eat dust all the days of your life. And I will put enmity between you and the woman, and between your offspring and hers; he will crush your head, and you will strike his heel."

God was not surprised nor caught without a remedy. Shortly after man's fall, he promises a future savior. God said, "I will put enmity between you (speaking to Satan) and the woman (Eve,) and between your offspring and hers." This shifts our focus. We move from the physical snake directly to Satan, the serpentine power behind the creature. (This is the same situation as when Jesus says to Peter, "Get behind me, Satan," rebuking the source of Peter's comment, rather than Peter, himself.) This evil one that has tempted mankind into destruction will be defeated, implying that things can be again as they once were.

Satan's destruction ("he will crush your head") will come at great pain to mankind's savior ("you will strike his heel".) Jesus pronounced Satan's defeat on the cross when he said "It is finished." The Greek word translated "finished" (John 19:30) was a business term for paid in full.

The pronoun, "he", tells us that the coming source of salvation—this "Offspring"—is a single person. It is not a segment of Eve's descendants, such as the nation of Israel. Odder yet, the word translated "offspring" or "seed" is the same as used for sperm, which women don't have. In fact, in the ancient view, the woman was considered merely an incubator of the life deposited in her by the male. Neither Adam nor his sons were to be involved in fathering this coming savior of man. (We find this lack of a human father stated in Matthew 1:18-25, Luke 1:26-38, and Galatians 4:4.)

TOTAL MANKIND'S SPIRITUAL DEATH
Genesis 3:19

By the sweat of your brow you will eat your food until you return to the ground, since from it you were taken; for dust you are and to dust you will return.

Now, the "breath of (spiritual) life" breathed into man earlier at his creation is gone. God says "dust you are..." which means man's life is now limited to physical life; spiritual life has gone.

Adam could not pass on to his children what he no longer had, thus, we are all born with only temporal life. All enter this world without the spiritual life God seeks to give.

Man separated himself from God, the source of life, and is therefore trapped in the death process unless rescued. The natural assumption of man is that life is his until God—or fate—wrongfully takes it. The truth is that man is in the process of a self-inflicted loss of life. Without God's intervention, the temporary survival we enjoy will flicker out. All of God's efforts attempt to rescue humankind; if he desired our damnation, he would have done nothing!

RECONCILIATION BY SUBSTITUTIONARY BLOOD
Genesis 3:21

The LORD God made garments of skin for Adam and his wife and clothed them.

Physical nakedness did not offend God when he clothed Adam and Eve with skins; he had made them naked. What had to be covered was their sins of disobedience, for no one can fellowship with God with their sins uncovered.

God then instituted a limited and temporary way by which humanity could periodically return to God's presence (3:21-24.) This was done by covering their sin (now a part of them) with the innocence of an animal. Clothed in the innocence of another, they could come back into a limited presence of God.

The word "atone" literally means to cover. All the future teaching in the Levitical law would deal with how man could get his sins "covered"—atoned—so he could come into God's fellowship. The focus of the Law would be in the requirement for Yom Kippur and Passover.

Though Moses recorded the specifics of Levitical sacrifice much later, they are written as if Israel was already familiar with the process.

Leviticus 7:8 makes a curious allowance as a part of the burnt offering. (The burnt offering was for the "covering" of deliberate sins.) The priest could do whatever he wished with the skin of the animal. Though it isn't stated, this continued the practice of burnt offerings as prescribed from man's earliest experience. In this earliest sacrifice, the priest was God himself and he used the skin to cover man's sins. God set the pattern at the beginning of man's separation. It is that our return to God can only occur by our sins being "covered"—atoned—by the blood on an innocent on our behalf.

Those sacrificial experiences before the sacrifice of Jesus were teaching tools. They were to prepare Israel to recognize the real thing when it came. John the Baptist did. Upon that recognition he said "Behold the Lamb of God, who takes away the sins of the world." (John 1:29)

RECONCILIATION ONLY BY SUBSTITUTIONARY BLOOD
Genesis 4:3-5

In the course of time Cain brought some of the fruits of the soil as an offering to the LORD. But Abel brought fat portions from some of the firstborn of his flock. The LORD looked with favor on Abel and is offering, but on Cain and his offering he did not look with favor.

At first reading it seems that God mistreats Cain in rejecting his offer of produce, but that isn't the case. Whatever else this teaches, it shows that God will accept no substitute for innocent blood as man's way back to him. Later, in the giving of the Levitical Law, he would be very specific. He would state in Leviticus 17:10, "...it is the blood that makes atonement for one's life."

When instituting the Lord's Supper, Jesus would later claim this role. He said—speaking of what the wine represented, "This is my blood of the covenant, which is poured out for the forgiveness of sins." (Matthew 26:28)

In the offerings of Cain and Abel, we have the basic conflict of mankind exemplified. It is whether man comes to God by his own efforts (works) or through the imputed innocence of another (grace.) The way of return into God's acceptance was already established, though we are not directly told so. It was—as instituted in the covering of Adam and Eve's sin—that man could only return through the atonement of shed blood. Able came to God that way. This time, Cain tried to come to God through the product of his work, his best crops (4:3-5.)

GOD'S COVENANT RE-ESTABLISHED
Genesis 9:11

"I will establish my covenant with you: Never again will there be a flood to destroy the earth."

Upon the exit of Noah and his family, God "re-established" his covenant with Noah. The content of the covenant, however, is never stated. The word most translate as "establish" means to "raise up," as when a flag has fallen. It suggests re-establishing more than initial creation. It must have been well known before the flood and was always (as later stated) "I will be your God and you will be my people."

God's basic covenant has never changed. Though he will expand it in unfolding history, it remains "I will be your God and you will be my people." (This is important! Rabbinic Judaism stresses that Gentiles are merely held accountable for the covenant given to Noah, while Jews stand under a higher one, that given to Moses. Thus, Christianity—which is considered idolatry for Jews—is considered acceptable for non-Jews because they are not held to as high a level of accountability.) The point to establish firmly is that there are **not** different covenants given by God. Rather, he gives expanded restatements of the same covenant: that **man is to depend on God, not self**. This even holds true of the "New Covenant" Jesus established as well.

EVE'S SEED TO COME THROUGH ABRAHAM'S LINE
Genesis 12:3

"I will bless those who bless you, and whoever curses you I will curse; and all peoples on earth will be blessed through you."

Genesis 26:4

"I will make your descendants as numerous as the stars in the sky and will give them all these lands. and through your offspring all nations on earth will be blessed..."

The story of Abram begins with his call. It is to leave all and go where God calls. God promised to make Abram prosperous, famous, and secure. Through him, God would bless the nations.
He expands that promise in Genesis 26:4 and passes it on to Jacob in 28:14.

Here God tells Abraham that he would have numerous descendants, but that this blessing would be the "offspring" promised to Eve.

Matthew 1:2 and Luke 3:34 agree that Jesus is a descendant of both Abraham and Jacob.

Abram was a man of faith, but it was not blind faith. He knew the basic covenant from what was received through those before him. (It was first given to Adam, in the warning not to trust self over God. God would later state this truth as, "I will be your God and you will be my people.")

Abram would have also known of the promise God made to Eve. He would have been familiar with the need to come to God through blood. He would have been familiar with God's restatement of the covenant to Noah and the removal of the curse on the ground.

SAVED BY FAITH
Genesis 15:6

Abram believed the LORD, and he credited it to him as righteousness.

This is a key verse! God has never changed. We must come to him just as Abraham did, that is, by **trust**. God commended Abraham for his trust, not his works. Rabbinic Judaism teaches that God chose Abraham because of his superior moral potential and that he earned his standing with God, though scripture says otherwise. The fact that we are only acceptable to God when we come trusting needs to be made as a principle that existed before the recording of the New Testament.

GOD TO PROVIDE THE SACRIFICE NEEDED FOR MAN
Genesis 22:1-19

Some time later God tested Abraham. He said to him, ..."Take your son, your only son, Isaac, whom you love, and go to the region of Moriah. Sacrifice him there as a burnt offering on one of the mountains I will tell you about."

...Abraham took the wood for the burnt offering and placed it on his son Isaac, and he himself carried the fire and the knife.

..."The fire and wood are here," Isaac said, "but where is the lamb for the burnt offering?"

Abraham answered, "God himself will provide the lamb for the burnt offering, my son." And the two of them went on together.

When they reached the place God had told him about, Abraham built an altar there and arranged the wood on it. He bound his son Isaac and laid him on the altar, on top of the wood. Then he reached out his hand and took the knife to slay his son.

But the angel of the LORD called out to him from heaven... "Do not lay a hand on the boy," he said. "Do not do anything to him...."

Abraham looked up and there in a thicket he saw a ram caught by its horns. He went over and took the ram and sacrificed it as a burnt offering instead of his son. So Abraham called that place The LORD Will Provide. And to this day it is said, "On the mountain of the LORD it will be provided."

It is better to use the obedience of Isaac as an illustration than as a prophecy of the Messiah. Isaac here is a **type** of Jesus, Abraham a type of the Father, the wood carried by Isaac reflecting the Cross. The point, however, is at the end of the story. Here Abraham utters a Messianic prophecy: "On the mountain of the Lord it (the needed sacrifice) will be provided."

Tradition holds this to be the mountain upon which Jerusalem sits, and thus, upon which the cross stood.

The predominant question about this passage deals with Abraham's expectancy (which Isaac must have shared) that God would keep his promise of descendants—and the special "seed"—**through** Isaac. God would do this, even if it took a resurrected Isaac.

John the Baptist would recognize this sacrificial role in Jesus by saying, "Behold, the Lamb of God." (John 1:35) The details of the fulfillment of this God given ram is in all of the crucifixion stories. (Matthew 26-28; Mark 14-16; Luke 22-24; John 18-20)

As man trusts God, God provides what man lacks. Truly, "God has provided his own sacrifice."

MESSIAH TO BE OF THE TRIBE OF JUDAH AND TO RULE THE WORLD
Genesis 49:10

The scepter will not depart from Judah, nor the ruler's staff from between his feet, until he comes to whom it belongs and the obedience of the nations is his.

As Jacob faces death, he gives a prophetic insight about each of the twelve tribes of Israel, headed by his sons. He says that national rule will reside in the tribe of Judah until it is established in the ultimate king. This is the king "whom the nations (the Gentiles) will obey."

The confusing point is over the world "Shiloh." Should we translate it as a proper name or as what it means? Either way the result is the same. The context shows that it is a reference is to a world-wide king, not the later location named Shiloh.

The complete fulfillment of the Messiah's rule is yet to come, but his coronation was on Palm Sunday (Matthew 21:1-11; Mark 11:1-11; Luke 19:28-44; John 12:12-19.)

Both Matthew (1:2) and Luke (3:34) declare Jesus to qualify as a descendant of Judah. Hebrews 7:14 and Revelation 5:5 tell us this is true.

THE PASSOVER FULFILLED IN THE CROSS
Exodus 12:1-51

...Take care of them until the fourteenth day of the month, when all the people of the community of Israel must slaughter them at twilight. Then they are to take some of the blood and put it on the sides and tops of the doorframes of the houses where they eat the lambs.... On that same night I will pass through Egypt and strike down every firstborn—both men and

animals—and I will bring judgment on all the gods of Egypt. I am the LORD.

The blood will be a sign for you on the houses where you are; and when I see the blood, I will pass over you. No destructive plague will touch you when I strike Egypt.

The loss of the first born looks back to Adam and forward to Jesus. The firstborn who died in each house represented the created "firstborn" of God, Adam. He, like Pharaoh, sought to be his own god and the result was death. That death, and its justice, would later be reflected in the requirement to redeem the firstborn son of each family. Israel was also required to redeem or kill the first born of any animal.

This death of the first born also looked forward to the time when the begotten "firstborn" of God, Jesus, would voluntarily die. This would pay the just death sentence of Adam and his descendants.

Specific protection came by the blood of the lamb placed on the sides and top of the door. Jesus, as the Lamb of God, provided that shed blood for us on the cross (John 19:34.)

THE DAY OF ATONEMENT FULFILLED IN THE CROSS
Leviticus 16

...From the Israelite community he is to take two male goats for a sin offering and a ram for a burnt offering. "Aaron is to offer the bull for his own sin offering to make atonement for himself and his household. Then he is to take the two goats and present them before the LORD at the entrance to the Tent of Meeting. He is to cast lots for the two goats—one lot for the LORD and the other for the scapegoat.

Aaron shall bring the goat whose lot falls to the LORD and sacrifice it for a sin offering. But the goat chosen by lot as the scape-goat shall be presented alive before the LORD to be used for making atonement by sending it into the desert as a scapegoat....

He shall then slaughter the goat for the sin offering for the people and take its blood behind the curtain and do with it as he did with the bull's blood .... He is to lay both hands on the head of the live goat and confess over it all the wickedness and rebellion of the Israelites—all

Jesus fulfilled Yom Kippur on the cross. First, he provided our entry into God's presence through his shed blood (John 19:34.) Second, he paid for our fallen nature by being our sin offering and for our rebellion as our burnt offering. Last, like the scape goat, he removed our sins. (You will find the record of this fulfillment in Matthew 27:35-46; Mark 15:20-26; Luke 23:11-35; and John 19:15-20:25.their sins—and put them on the goat's head. He shall send the goat away into the desert in the care of a man appointed for the task....

Then Aaron is to go into the Tent of Meeting and take off the linen garments he put on before he entered the Most Holy Place, and he is to leave them there. He shall bathe himself with water in a holy place and put on his regular garments. Then he shall come out and sacrifice the burnt offering for himself and the burnt offering for the people, to make atonement for himself and for the people....

SAVED BY FAITH
Numbers 21:6-9

Then the LORD sent venomous snakes among them; they bit the people and many Israelites died. The people came to Moses and said, "We sinned when we spoke against the

LORD and against you. Pray that the LORD will take the snakes away from us." So Moses prayed for the people.

The LORD said to Moses, "Make a snake and put it up on a pole; anyone who is bitten can look at it and live." So Moses made a bronze snake and put it up on a pole. Then when anyone was bitten by a snake and looked at the bronze snake, he lived.

Again, we have a God given illustration of a coming truth. Jesus confirms this in John 3:14, where he compares himself to the bronze serpent. The principle is that we are saved by trusting God's way —no matter how foolish it seems to mankind—rather than our own capacity to beat death. Ephesians 2:8-9 records the same truth.

A PROPHET GREATER THAN MOSES
Deuteronomy 18:15-19

The LORD your God will raise up for you a prophet like me from among your own brothers. You must listen to him. For this is what you asked of the LORD your God at Horeb on the day of the assembly when you said, "Let us not hear the voice of the LORD our God nor see this great fire anymore, or we will die."

The LORD said to me: "What they say is good. I will raise up for them a prophet like you from among their brothers; I will put my words in his mouth, and he will tell them everything I command him. If anyone does not listen to my words that the prophet speaks in my name, I myself will call him to account.

The point to make is that God says this prophet **must** be obeyed. His requirements are more compulsory than the Law.

Many of Jesus' day viewed him as "the prophet." (John 7:40) Later, in his Pentecost sermon, Peter would affirm that Jesus fulfilled this prophecy (Acts 3;20-26.) His superiority to Moses is the subject of Hebrews 3.

AN ETERNAL KINGDOM OF DAVID'S DYNASTY
II Samuel 7:16—also in I Kings 9:5

"Your house and your kingdom will endure forever before me; your throne will be established forever.

God had already promised that the Messiah's rule would reach beyond the borders of Israel. Later, the promise to David, repeated to Solomon, is that this kingdom will also be unlimited by time.

The last (and eternal) king in this dynasty was proclaimed king on Palm Sunday (Matthew 21:1-11; Mark 11:1-11; Luke 19:28-44; John 12:12-19.) Luke 1:32-33 and Acts 13:22-23 record that Jesus was that king.

THE ETERNAL KING TO BE GOD'S ANOINTED
Psalm 2:1-8

Why do the nations conspire and the peoples plot in vain?

The kings of the earth take their stand and the rulers gather together against the LORD and against his Anointed One. "Let us break their chains," they say, "and throw off their fetters."

The One enthroned in heaven laughs; the Lord scoffs at them. Then he rebukes them in his anger and terrifies them in his

wrath, saying, "I have installed my King on Zion, my holy hill." I will proclaim the decree of the LORD: He said to me, "You are my Son; today I have become your Father. Ask of me, and I will make the nations your inheritance, the ends of the earth your possession.

This psalm forces us to ask, "Does this refer to David, or to a coming king?" The answer seems to be both. However, the major fulfillment seems to reach beyond David's world. For example, in verse two we find the opposition to be religious, not political. David's enemies were political, not religious. Here, however, the opposition is against God first, and incidentally against the Messiah.

Christians have no problem seeing Jesus foretold here, but those still seeking to find another way to salvation may not see it that clearly. If not, the major point is still that this Psalm identifies the special king and prophet of which we have earlier heard. Here he is literally called, "Messiah," the Anointed One.

MAN'S RESURRECTION PROMISED
Psalm 16:9-10

Therefore my heart is glad and my tongue rejoices; my body also will rest secure, because you will not abandon me to the grave, nor will you let your Holy One see decay.

David here claims God's promise to raise him from the dead. He expects to die physically, but not to be left in "Sheol." He prophecies that death cannot touch someone else. That other person is God's "Holy One," who will not see decay.

Today, in Jerusalem, you can visit David's decaying bones, but not those of the "Holy One." Even the angels proclaimed "He is Risen!" Matthew 28:1-15; Mark 16:1-8; Luke 24:1-53; and John 20:1-21:25 give the full resurrection record. In his Pentecost sermon (Acts 2:22-

41,) Peter uses this very verse in proclaiming Jesus' resurrection.

THE CRUCIFIXION
Psalms 22:1-18

My God, my God, why have you forsaken me? Why are you so far from saving me, so far from the words of my groaning? O my God, I cry out by day, but you do not answer, by night, and am not silent.

Yet you are enthroned as the Holy One; you are the praise of Israel. In you our fathers put their trust; they trusted and you delivered them. They cried to you and were saved; in you they trusted and were not disap-pointed.

But I am a worm and not a man, scorned by men and despised by the people. All who see me mock me; they hurl insults, shaking their heads: "He trusts in the LORD; let the LORD rescue him. Let him deliver him, since he delights in him."

...My strength is dried up like a potsherd, and my tongue sticks to the roof of my mouth; you lay me in the dust of death. Dogs have surrounded me; a band of evil men has encircled me, they have pierced my hands and my feet. I can count all my bones; people stare and gloat over me. They divide my garments among them and cast lots for my clothing.

In the initial part of the Psalm, David seems to recount suffering in his life. It seems this is an experiential prophecy of the agony of Jesus on the cross. Jesus' cry from the cross, "My God, my God, why have you forsaken me?" is either a quote from the beginning of this psalm, or else David foretells what Jesus would later say. Jesus' loneliness and abandonment at that hour is reflected in David's cry of abandonment.

Later in the Psalm, he recounts experiences that would be a part of the cross that are beyond coincidence. In verse 16 and 17 we have Jesus' death by crucifixion foretold. Only crucifixion, which didn't exit in David's day, would cause pierced hands and feet. We also read that Jesus would suffer no broken bones, though the thieves who died with him had their legs broken for quicker death. Even the division of his only worldly goods, his clothing, by lots is foretold.

Even more prophetic, David changes from first person ("I") to third person ("he") in verse 24. Now we see clearly that David is speaking of someone other than himself. He praises this one who has suffered and identifies him as the coming King whose borders are limitless and whose rule is eternal.

You will find the record of this fulfillment in Matthew 27:35-46; Mark 15:20-26; Luke 23:11-35; and John 19:15-20:25.

MESSIAH TO BE (1) A KING SUPERIOR TO DAVID, (2) A PRIEST SUPERIOR TO AARON, AND (3) A JUDGE SUPERIOR TO MOSES
Psalm 110:1-7

The LORD (Jehovah) says to my Lord (master): "Sit at my right hand until I make your enemies a foot-stool for your feet." The LORD will extend your mighty scepter from Zion; you will rule in the midst of your enemies. Your troops will be willing on your day of battle. Arrayed in holy majesty, from the womb of the dawn you will receive the dew of your youth.

The LORD has sworn and will not change his mind: "You are a priest forever, in the order of Melchizedek."

The Lord is at your right hand; he will crush kings on the day of his wrath. He will judge the nations, heaping up the dead and crushing the rulers of the whole earth. He will drink from a brook beside the way; therefore he will lift up his head.

Sadly, Bible translators follow an established Jewish tradition of translating Jehovah in most cases as "Lord." "Lord" is also used for the words meaning "Sir," or "Master," which can apply to others as well. When the world "Lord" is really Jehovah, the word is printed in upper case letters, though they are smaller than normal capitals. This is the case here. Verse one literally begins, "My Lord (Jehovah) says to my Lord (master): Sit at my right hand until I make your enemies your footstool."

Jehovah will elevate the one to whom David speaks and calls "Master." He will enjoy a three-fold position of: (1) an expanded rule, (2) an eternal priesthood, and (3) the ultimate judgment of mankind.

This will be a king superior to David, for David—of whose line he descends—calls him "Lord."

He will also be a priest superior to the current Levitical priesthood. He will be like "Melchizedek." Melchizedek appears in Israel's history in Genesis 14:18-20. Hebrews 7 gives the best explanation of this role.

Last, Moses was the ultimate judge of Israel. This coming "Lord" of David will judge not only Israel, but all nations.

His rule has begun (Luke 24:50-51; Acts 2:23-36; Revelation 5:11-14;) his intercession as priest continues (see Hebrews 10:1-14;) and his judgment awaits the world (Revelation 19:11-21.)

MESSIAH TO BE REJECTED BY ISRAEL'S LEADERS
Psalm 118:22-23

The stone the builders rejected has become the capstone; the LORD has done this, and it is marvelous in our eyes.

Basically this is a psalm of praise for God's faithful deliverance of David.

However, in this proclamation of God's goodness, David adds a line that seems to be an afterthought about God's ways. It is "The stone the builders rejected has become the capstone; the Lord (Jehovah) has done this..."

The capstone or keystone in an arch is the most critical stone. It gives balance so the arch stands. That keystone of what God is building will be rejected by those whose job it is to built the arch. The builders are the religious leaders of Israel.

John laments the truth of that fact in John 1:11-12 when he says of God, the Word, "He came unto his own, but his own would not receive him...." The specific rejection of the Jewish leaders, not the people, is recorded in places like John 12:37-43 and Acts 4;1-12.

THE MESSIANIC AGE TO COME
Isaiah 2:2-4

In the last days the mountain of the LORD'S temple will be established as chief among the nations; it will be raised above the hills, and all nations will stream to it. Many people will come and say, "Come, let us go up to the mountain of the LORD, to the house of the God of Jacob. He will teach us his ways, so that we may walk in his paths."

The law will go out from Zion, the word of the LORD from Jerusalem. He will judge between the nations and will settle disputes for many peoples. They will beat their swords into plowshares and their spears into pruning hooks. Nation will not take up sword against nation, nor will they train for war anymore.

Isaiah 4:2

In that day the Branch of the LORD will be beautiful and glorious...

Isaiah uses an analogy of ultimate power for the Messiah—"the mountain" of the Lord. God will later clearly identify this "mountain", in Daniel 2:44, as the unending kingdom of God. Chapter 4 gives us a new term for the Messiah: the Branch of the Lord. This will recur and be expanded later in Isaiah.

The challenge of Isaiah 2:2-4 is not whether it is Messianic or not, but whether Jesus fulfills it or not. Rabbinic Judaism says that this proves Jesus couldn't have been the Messiah because peace has not come to man. The key to that is that Isaiah says that this will occur "in the last days," not in the Messiah's first appearing.

MESSIAH'S VIRGIN BIRTH
Isaiah 7:13-14

Then Isaiah said, "Hear now, you house of David! Is it not enough to try the patience of men? Will you try the patience of my God also? Therefore the LORD himself will give you a sign: The virgin will be with child and will give birth a son, and will call him Immanuel ....

The hint to Eve is now clearly stated. Skeptics try to explain this verse away. They claim we should translate "virgin" as "maiden" or "young girl." They also try to find its fulfillment in the days of Isaiah, eliminating its need for fulfillment in later times.

The Hebrew term, "almah," which is translated virgin, does literally mean maiden, not virgin. The problem is that no Hebrew word for virgin exists; it is assumed that a maiden would be a virgin. This was the translation by Israel's religious leaders before Rabbinic Judaism.

When the Hebrew scripture was translated into Greek, the Greek language had a specific word for virgin. Thus, they translated "almah" as the Greek word for virgin, rather than the Greek for young maiden. Also, Song of Songs 6:8 shows us that "almah" should be understood as sexually uninitiated. It gives three classes of women; queens, concubines, and virgins—"almahs." Queens and concubines—whatever their age—are divided by their position in the King's household, not by their use as sex objects. Concubines were servants who also served according to the King's pleasure, sexually. Why would those referred to as "almahs" (virgins) be segregated from the other female servants—concubines—except that they were (at least to that point) exempt from sexual service?

The weak argument for the fulfillment of this prophecy in Isaiah's time—assuming that you remove the virgin-birth limitations—argues that Jesus was born to late to fulfill it. The timing however is that the deliverance of Jerusalem from the king's feared enemies would come **before** this child was born. Skeptics then look for fulfillment in a child born shortly after the siege is lifted. Their candidates have little to prove they are that child and certainly don't qualify as "Immanuel," God with us! But what of the time? It doesn't say the child will come one day after, or a million years after the lifting of this siege. He just comes **after**, which Jesus did!

The Greek scripture (New Testament) is very clear that Jesus had no earthly father, and that he was "God with us"—Immanuel. Again, the fulfillment is recorded in Matthew 1:18-25, Luke 1:26-38, and Galatians 4:4.

MESSIAH TO BE BOTH GOD AND MAN
Isaiah 9:6-7

For to us a child is born, to us a son is given, and the government will be on his shoulders. And he will be called

Wonderful Counselor, Mighty God, Everlasting Father, Prince of Peace.

Of the increase of his government and peace there will be no end. He will reign on David's throne and over his kingdom, establishing and upholding it with justice and righteousness from that time on and forever. The zeal of the LORD Almighty will accomplish this.

Here, we have a new quality of the coming great King. Isaiah says, "unto us a child is born," showing that he is about to speak about a coming Jewish child who would be a ruler of Israel. So far, so good. Then he identifies him as "Mighty God." (The Hebrew is "El Gibbor," which Jeremiah says is Jehovah.) He is also the Everlasting (only God is everlasting) Father—though he has already said he would be human, specifically Jewish.

Then lest we should miss it, he states categorically in verse 7, that this God-man child would be the expected eternal King.

Luke records the explanation of Gabriel to Mary of her pending pregnancy by explaining that Jesus will be this God-man. We also find this claim in Acts 13:22-23. Philippians 2:6-8 is the view of the same event from heaven's perspective.

THE MESSIAH'S CHARACTER
Isaiah 11:1-9

A shoot will come up from the stump of Jesse; from his roots a Branch will bear fruit. The Spirit of the LORD will rest on him—the Spirit of wisdom and of understanding, the Spirit of counsel and of power, the Spirit of knowledge and of the fear of the LORD—and he will delight in the fear of the LORD. He will not judge by what he sees with his eyes, or decide by what he hears with his ears; but with righteousness he will judge the needy, with justice he will give decisions for the poor of the earth. He will strike the earth with the rod of his mouth; with the breath of his lips he will slay the wicked. Righteousness will be his belt and faithfulness the sash around his waist....

Isaiah identifies "the Branch" which he earlier said would rule as a descendant of Jesse (the father of David.) The Messiah's character and ultimate kingdom is then described. Total fulfill-meant of a kingdom of peace is yet to come, but the life of Jesus qualifies him as to character. The four gospels all reflect this, but perhaps a specific place to test Jesus' values against these verses would be the Beatitudes (Matthew 5:1-10.)

MESSIAH'S FOLLOWERS TO BE JEW AND GENTILE
Isaiah 11:10-11

In that day the Root of Jesse will stand as a banner for the peoples; the nations will rally to him, and his place of rest will be glorious. In that day the Lord will reach out his hand a second time to reclaim the remnant that is left of his people...

Here, and in other prophecies, the Messiah transcends Israel. He is the king for all mankind. History has fulfilled this prophecy as the nations have rallied to him.

MAN'S RESURRECTION TO BE PROVIDED BY GOD
Isaiah 25:7-8

On this mountain he will destroy the shroud that enfolds all peoples, the sheet that covers all nations; he will swallow up death forever. The Sovereign LORD will wipe away the tears from all faces; he will remove the disgrace of his people from all the earth. The LORD has spoken.

God promises that "on this mountain" (Jerusalem) he will destroy death. That destruction of death was proclaimed when the angel chided Mary with the words, Why are you seeking the living among the dead?" The proof of God's plan for our resurrection is that of Jesus (Matthew 28:1-15; Mark 16:1-8; Luke 24:1-53; and John 20:1-21:25.)

MESSIAH TO WORK MIRACLES
Isaiah 35:4-6

Say to those with fearful hearts, "Be strong, do not fear; your God will come, he will come with vengeance; with divine retribution he will come to save you."

Then will the eyes of the blind be opened and the ears of the deaf unstopped. Then will the lame leap like a deer, and the mute tongue shout for joy. Water will gush forth in the wilderness and streams in the desert.

The promise is that when God comes, he will bring retribution to some and salvation to others. In that coming, the blind will see, the deaf hear, and the lame walk. These accounts fill the gospels. Perhaps the best example is the report that Jesus said to take to John the Baptist, recorded in Matthew 11:4-6.

A MESSENGER TO PRECEDE THE MESSIAH
Isaiah 40:3

A voice of one calling: "In the desert prepare the way for the LORD; make straight in the wilderness a highway for our God.

This was John the Baptist. (Matthew 3;1-3; Mark 1:1-8; Luke 1:7; John 1:23)

THE SERVANT OF THE LORD

Who is the servant of the Lord? Well, it depends. The rabbis teach that passages about the "servant of the Lord" refer to the Jewish people. Christians see Jesus as the "servant." In some places, the servant is Israel and in some it is the coming Messiah. Distinguish between these and show that those referring to the Messiah could not be fulfilled by the nation, Israel.

Isaiah 41:8-9

"But you, O Israel, my servant, Jacob, whom I have chosen, you descendants of Abraham my friend, I took you from the ends of the earth, from its farthest corners I called you. I said, 'You are my servant'; I have chosen you and have not rejected you.

Isaiah 42:18-19

"Hear, you deaf; look, you blind, and see! Who is blind but my servant, and deaf like the messenger I send? Who is blind like the one committed to me, blind like the servant of the LORD?

Isaiah 43:8-10

Lead out those who have eyes but are blind, who have ears but are deaf. All the nations gather together and the peoples assemble. Which of them foretold this and proclaimed to us the former things? Let them bring in their witnesses to prove they were right, so that others may hear and say, "It is true."

"You are my witnesses," declares the LORD, "and my servant whom I have chosen, so that you may know and believe me and understand that I am he. Before me no god was formed, nor will there be one after me.

Isaiah 44:1-5

"But now listen, O Jacob, my servant, Israel, whom I have chosen. This is what the LORD says—he who made you, who formed you in the womb, and who will help you: Do not be afraid, O Jacob, my servant, Jeshurun, whom I have chosen.

For I will pour water on the thirsty land, and streams on the dry ground; I will pour out my Spirit on your offspring, and my blessing on your descendants. They will spring up like grass in a meadow, like poplar trees by flowing streams.

One will say, 'I belong to the LORD'; another will call himself by the name of Jacob; still another will write on his hand, 'The LORD's,' and will take the name Israel.

ISRAEL AS SERVANT

Having told the Gentiles to not gloat over Israel's being disciplined, God then contrasts their role to that of the other nations. He speaks to Israel and assures them that they have not been abandoned, that God has not revoked their calling, that they are "Israel, my servant." (Isaiah 41:8-9)

The key to understanding the "service" they are chosen to give is in 43:12: "You are my witnesses...that I am God." In the role of world evangelization, Israel will always have a predominant place. This is not preferential treatment but a fact of their history. No other people can give testimony of the truth of God out of their own national experience. Throughout this section (40:1-51:16) God uses the proof we must use as our authority. **TAKE NOTE!** He stakes his veracity on his ability to predict coming events, perfectly. He then encourages Israel to trust him for this future purpose and then condemns them for trusting in other gods. He then presents his case (41:21-29.) Israel, however, failed to trust this infallible truth.

In this failure of faith, the national servant of God developed an adulterous affair with the gods of the nations. The verdict is given in verse 29: "See, they are all false! Their deeds amount to nothing; their images are but wind and confusion." This is a much different description than the servant of God in Chapter 42.

In 43:8-10, Israel is identified as a blind and deaf servant; blind and deaf by their own choice. They are also castigated by God as stubborn and rebellious in 48:1-11. This not their final condition, for God continually promises restoration. (Isaiah 44:1-5)

Isaiah 42:1-9

"Here is my servant, whom I uphold, my chosen one in whom I delight; I will put my Spirit on him and he will bring justice to the nations. He will not shout or cry out, or raise his voice in the streets. A bruised reed he will not break, and a smoldering wick he will not snuff out. In faithfulness he will bring forth justice; he will not falter or be discouraged till he establishes justice on earth. In his law the islands will put their hope."

This is what God the LORD says...I will keep you and will make you to be a covenant for the people and a light for the Gentiles, to open eyes that are blind, to free captives from prison and to release from the dungeon those who sit in darkness.

Isaiah 49:1-26

And now the LORD says— he who formed me in the womb to be his servant to bring Jacob back to him and gather Israel to himself, for I am honored in the eyes of the LORD and my God has been my strength—he says: "It is too small a thing for you to be my servant to restore the tribes of Jacob and bring back those of Israel I have kept. I will also make you a light for the Gentiles, that you may bring my salvation to the ends of the earth."

THE MESSIAH AS SERVANT

We are justified in looking to a different person because the description here differs from that of Israel which God has just given. This becomes more and more evident as the portrait unfolds.

The critical key is in 49:5, where the purpose of this servant is given: "...to be his servant to **bring Jacob back** to him and gather Israel to himself..." The purpose of this faithful servant is to retrieve a faithless national servant. They two can not be the same thing.

The two qualities that Israel most fails to fulfill are that this servant will bring forth justice in faithfulness and be the hope of the Gentiles. Faithfulness has never been a quality of Israel! In fact, Israel's faithlessness is stated repeatedly.

Even if today's Rabbinic Judaism were the correct way to worship God for the Jewish people, the vast bulk are non-practicing. There is no escape from the fact that the majority have been faithless, both in the past and in the present. (Please note! You must not let your friend think you are claiming a greater faithfulness to God for non-Jews. Make the point that non-Jews, including Christians, have been no more faithful to God than the Jewish people. That's why grace is so important for both.)

In Isaiah 42:6-7, we find that this servant is to be a "covenant" for the people (Israel) and a light for the Gentiles, to open eyes that are blind (Israel, the blind servant of 42:19,) to free captives from prison and to release ...those who sit in darkness (Gentiles.)"

This servant is to be a "light" for those who "sit in darkness." Israel had possessed God's light for generations; the nations had not. The Gentile problem is stated as lack of light. Israel's problem was blindness to the light that existed in their midst. This servant will bring deliverance from both kinds of darkness.

The logic of this comparison is to show that God is now speaking of two servants; the faithless, deaf and blind servant (42:18-20,) and this servant who brings light to the Gentiles and sight to the Jews.

Jesus identified himself as this servant in Luke 4:21 and lived a life exemplifying these qualities. Some examples of these qualities being fulfilled in Jesus include his being anointing with power (Luke 4:14) and his meekness (Matthew 12:17-21; 26:47-56.)

Isaiah 49 expands on the description of the second servant. In 49:3, this servant is identified as "my servant, Israel." How then can we assert that this is not the national servant, but rather the servant Messiah, in the face of the literal words?

Again, 49:5 gives the purpose of this servant as being the source of redemption for the national servant, Israel; therefore, they can't be the same entity. How though do we explain the use of "Israel" for the servant Messiah? The national purpose is fulfilled through individuals. All that Israel was to accomplish, past and future, is in reality accomplished through the power of her divine-human son, Jesus the Messiah. For more than the Jewish people, it is in the Messiah that God says, "**You** are my servant, Israel, **in whom** I will display my splendor."

Finally, in chapter 50 the two servants are contrasted. Israel's sins are stated in verses 1-3. The faithfulness of the Messiah servant is listed in verses 4-9. The fulfillment of his refusal to rebel against God's plan is given in Matthew 17:11-14. His being mocked, spit upon and beaten are recorded in Matthew 26:17 and 27:26.

ISAIAH'S VIEW OF THE CROSS

When we read Isaiah 52:13-53:12, we wonder how anyone can miss this picture of Jesus. However, it is not a passage that Rabbinic Judaism has missed. If your friend has not talked to his rabbi about it, he most likely will. How then does Judaism explain this passage without bumping into Jesus? They do so, by claiming that the suffering servant is the nation, Israel, not an individual.

Here is a suggestion on how to share this passage. First, read the whole passage together for the general picture. Then either read or tell the story of the Ethiopian eunuch and his question of Philip as he read this passage (Acts 8:32-34.) Say, "His question—'Who is the prophet talking about?'—needs to be our first question."

What points to this being a coming individual, rather than the nation Israel? (Always, make your strongest irrefutable point first, and then affirm it with the weaker proofs.) The arguments against seeing Israel as this servant are in verses 7-9. The strongest argument against this view is in verse eight, "...for the transgression (the sins) of my people (Israel,) he (the servant) was stricken." Israel can't be both.

Second, though innocent, the servant dies a voluntary, substitutionary death. There is no arguing the fact that the Jewish people have suffered unjustly, but they fail to qualify as being without guilt before God. Neither have they ever suffered voluntarily.

Further, the Rabbinic view of the Jewish servant role is to be God's model of morality for the balance of mankind. They see their suffering as anti-Semitic attempts to eliminate them as the world's moral example. However, the passage says that the suffering comes at the hand of God, not evil men. Also, Israel shares the guilt of mankind and deserved the punishment inflicted on the servant. She is not an innocent, suffering because of her pure moral example.

More importantly, from a Biblical perspective, Isaiah and Jeremiah identify the coming eternal King as the righteous "Branch." (Isaiah 11:1-9; Jeremiah 23:5-6) Zechariah 3:8 identifies the "Branch" as God's servant. Things equal to the same thing are equal to each other in logic as well as geometry. Thus, the suffering servant is Israel's coming eternal king, not Israel, herself.

MESSIAH GLORIFIED IN THE CROSS
Isaiah 52:13

See, my servant will act wisely; he will be raised and lifted up and highly exalted.

In one sense Jesus was exalted on Palm Sunday, but the "lifting up" that exalted him was the cross (John 12:23-32.)

MAN DIVIDED INTO TWO CAMPS
Isaiah 52:14-15

Just as there were many who were appalled at him—his appearance was so disfigured beyond that of any man and his form marred beyond human likeness—so will he sprinkle many nations, and kings will shut their mouths because of him. For what they were not told, they will see, and what they have not heard, they will understand.

People are either appalled by him or attracted to him. The reference to his disfigured physical appearance is found in his beating preceding the crucifixion (John 19:1-3.) The point, however, is that he will repel those who only see him as human. Those who see beyond his humanity, will be drawn to him. This is one of many verses dealing with the vast following of non-Jews that the Jewish Messiah will have. The vast number of International Christians is the fulfillment of, "what they were not told, they will see, and what they have not heard, they will understand." Though the Gentiles lacked Israel's background, they would come to her Messiah. (Romans 9:30-33)

MESSIAH TO BE BROADLY REJECTED
Isaiah 53:1

Who has believed our message and to whom has the arm of the LORD been revealed?

Even with miracles done before them, many did not believe Jesus. John 12:37-38 is the direct record of the fulfillment of this verse.

MESSIAH TO BE VIRGIN BORN
Isaiah 53:2a

He grew up before him like a tender shoot, and like a root out of dry ground.

This is not the major verse upon which to build the case for the Messiah's virgin birth, but seems to support it. "Land" is often a symbol of Israel and moisture was a euphemism in the Jewish culture for male sperm.

Nonetheless, this servant is to grow before God, just as we find recorded of Jesus in Luke 2:40.

MESSIAH TO BE BROADLY REJECTED
Isaiah 53:2b-3

He had no beauty or majesty to attract us to him, nothing in his appearance that we should desire him. He was despised and rejected by men, a man of sorrows, and familiar with suffering. Like one from whom men hide their faces he was despised, and we esteemed him not.

Again, the servant will have no physical appeal. The record of this is in John 1:11 and 7:47-48.

MESSIAH TO BE A SACRIFICE FOR MAN'S SINS
Isaiah 53:4-6

Surely he took up our infirmities and carried our sorrows, yet we considered him stricken by God, smitten by him, and afflicted. But he was pierced for our transgressions, he was crushed for our iniquities; the punishment that brought us peace was upon him, and by his wounds we are healed.

We all, like sheep, have gone astray, each of us has turned to his own way; and the LORD has laid on him the iniquity of us all.

The Messiah would suffer for Israel's weaknesses, but most would think it was God's punishment of him. However, his punishment would not be for his sins, but would bring reconciliation between man and God.

John the Baptist would recognize that role, early in Jesus' ministry (John 1:29.) Caiaphas, the High Priest, would unknowingly prophesy that Jesus should fill such a role (John 11:47-52.) Paul would later make this the center of his message. (I Corinthians 15:3)

THE MESSIAH TO DIE VOLUNTARILY
Isaiah 53:7

He was oppressed and afflicted, yet he did not open his mouth; he was led like a lamb to the slaughter, and as a sheep before her shearers is silent, so he did not open his mouth.

Jesus chose not to defend himself, throughout the whole process. (Matthew 26:59-63; 27:12-14; Mark 15:3-5; and Luke 23:8-9)

MESSIAH TO BE UNJUSTLY CONDEMNED
Isaiah 53:8

By oppression and judgment he was taken away. And who can speak of his descendants? For he was cut off from the land of the living; for the transgression of my people he was stricken.

We find a growing plan to condemn Jesus before his trial ever began. The Sanhedrin convened court illegally, and its witnesses lied. (Matthew 26:59-68, 27:1-2; Luke 23;1-25)

MESSIAH TO BE BURIED IN A RICH MAN'S GRAVE
Isaiah 53:9

He was assigned a grave with the wicked, and with the rich in his death, though he had done no violence, nor was any deceit in his mouth.

We find the specific fulfillment of this in Matthew 27:57-60; Mark 15:42-47; and Luke 23:50-52.

MESSIAH'S RESURRECTION PROMISED
Isaiah 53:10

Yet it was the LORD's will to crush him and cause him to suffer, and though the LORD makes his life a guilt offering, he will see his offspring and prolong his days, and the will of the LORD will prosper in his hand.

The Messiah is to be Jehovah's guilt offering but will survive and accomplish God's will. Hebrews 2:10 records his success.

MESSIAH PROVIDES FOR MAN'S JUSTIFICATION
Isaiah 53:11-12

After the suffering of his soul, he will see the light and be satisfied; by his knowledge my righteous servant will justify many, and he will bear their iniquities. Therefore, I will give him a portion among the great, and he will divide the spoils with the strong, because he poured out his life unto death, and was numbered with the transgressors. For he bore the sin of many, and made intercession for the transgressors.

Man was to be made right with God by the servant's justification, not his own. (Luke 23:32-22; Romans 3:22-24; Ephesians 2:8-9; Hebrews 9:26,28; I Peter 3:18)

THE KING WHO IS THE RIGHTEOUS BRANCH
Jeremiah 23:5-6

"The days are coming," declares the LORD, "when I will raise up to David a righteous Branch, a King who will reign wisely and do what is just and right in the land. In his days Judah will be saved and Israel will live in safety. This is the name by which he will be called: The LORD Our Righteousness.

Jeremiah speaks of the coming king of David who will be God's shepherd. He is the "Righteous Branch." Jesus would claim to be that shepherd in John 10:7-17.

THE NEW COVENANT
Jeremiah 31:31

"The time is coming," declares the LORD, "when I will make a new covenant with the house of Israel and with the house of Judah.

Though the thought that anything could be superior to the covenant given to Moses is abhorrent to Rabbinic thinking, God's promise is exactly that! Note...this doesn't say that the existing covenant was abandoned. Rather, this is the promise of an addition which is an improvement. (Matthew 26:17, 27-29; Luke 22:15-20; Romans 11:26-27; Hebrews 8:6-13; 9:12-22; 10;4-14)

THE GOOD SHEPHERD
Ezekiel 34:11,23

For this is what the Sovereign LORD says: "I myself will search for my sheep and look after them. ...I will place over them one shepherd, my servant David, and he will tend them; he will tend them and be their shepherd.

God claims he will be the shepherd and that the shepherd will be a descendant of David. Jesus would later say in John 10:7-17 that he is that shepherd.

EXACT TIME OF THE MESSIAH'S COMING
Daniel 9:24-27

"Seventy 'sevens' are decreed for your people and your holy city to finish transgression, to put an end to sin, to atone for wicked-ness, to bring in everlasting righteousness, to seal up vision and prophecy and to anoint the most holy.

"Know and understand this: From the issuing of the decree to restore and rebuild Jerusalem until the Anointed One, the ruler, comes, there will be seven 'sevens,' and sixty-two 'sevens.' It will be rebuilt with streets and a trench, but in times of trouble.

If Jesus wasn't the Messiah, **everyone** has missed him, because his time to come ran out almost 2,000 years ago! These verses say that Messiah is to come 483 years (7x7 + 62x7) after the decree to rebuilt Jerusalem. Cyrus of Persia gave that decree in 536 B.C. Remember that we don't have a complete calendar that goes back to Cyrus, but whatever the unknown gap was, the Messiah has already come.

GENTILES INCLUDED IN REDEMPTIVE PLAN
Hosea 1:10

"Yet the Israelites will be like the sand on the seashore, which cannot be measured or counted. In the place where it was said to them, 'You are not my people,' they will be called 'sons of the living God.'

Paul speaks of this in Romans 9:22-25.

MESSIAH BURIED THREE DAYS, LIKE JONAH
Jonah 1:17

But the LORD provided a great fish to swallow Jonah, and Jonah was inside the fish three days and three nights.

Jesus declares that the three days and nights the prophet Jonah spent in the great fish was a sign of his coming time in the grave. (Matthew 12:29-42)

MESSIAH TO BE BORN IN BETHLEHEM
Micah 5:2

"But you, Bethlehem Ephrathah, though you are small among the clans of Judah, out of you will come for me one who will be ruler over Israel, whose origins are from of old, from ancient times."

This ruler of Israel will be a ruler who is God (from ancient time) and man. (Matthew 2;1-6; Luke 2:4-7)

RIGHTEOUS KING TO ENTER JERUSALEM ON A COLT
Zechariah 9:9

Rejoice greatly, O Daughter of Zion! Shout, Daughter of Jerusalem! See, your king comes to you, righteous and having salvation, gentle and riding on a donkey, on a colt, the foal of a donkey.

Jesus fulfilled this on Palm Sunday. (Matthew 21:1-9; Mark 11:1-11; Luke 19:28-40; John 12:12-15)

POTTER'S FIELD BOUGHT WITH PRICE OF GOOD SHEPHERD
Zechariah 11:12-13

I told them, "If you think it best, give me my pay; but if not, keep it." So they paid me thirty pieces of silver. And the LORD said to me, "Throw it to the potter"—the handsome price at which they priced me! So I took the thirty pieces of silver and threw them into the house of the LORD to the potter.

This was fulfilled with the return of the 30 pieces of silver to the Temple by Judas. Because it was blood money, they used it to buy a cemetery for the outcasts. (Matthew 27:3-10)

ISRAEL'S COMING RECOGNITION OF THE MESSIAH
Zechariah 12:10

"And I will pour out on the house of David and the inhabitants of Jerusalem a spirit of grace and supplication.

They will look on me, the one they have pierced, and they will mourn for him as one mourns for an only child, and grieve bitterly for him as one grieves for a firstborn son.

Here is a promise of a day to come when the Jewish people will recognize Jesus as the Messiah. Their grief will be over their failure to have done so earlier.

A MESSENGER TO PRECEDE THE MESSIAH
Malachi 3:1

"See, I will send my messenger, who will prepare the way before me. Then suddenly the Lord you are seeking will come

to his temple; the messenger of the covenant, whom you desire, will come," says the LORD Almighty.

This is John the Baptist. (Matthew 3;1-3; Mark 1:1-8; Luke 1:7; John 1:23)

SAVED BY FAITH
John 3:16

For God so loved the world that he gave his one and only Son, that whoever believes in him shall not perish but have eternal life.

The critical point to convey is that the human part of the salvation process is **trust**. A good way to share it is by amplifying it. You cay say, "The Bible says, 'For God so loved the world'... that's you and me, not the dirt...'that he gave his only begotten son'... Jesus, who was God who became a man...'that whosoever'...tall or short, good or bad...'believed in him would not perish'...that is, not spend eternity in Hell cut off from God...'but have everlasting life'...which is to live perfectly, forever."

A way to illustrate the trust is as follows: "Do you know what it means to believe in him? It isn't just knowing Jesus was who he claimed to be. Satan knows that and he isn't saved. To believe in him means to depend on him—like you would a doctor. When you are sick, you go to one you "believe in." You put yourself in his hands and whether live or die depends on him. God promises that when we put ourselves in the hands of Jesus—and depend on him in the same way—he will guarantee that we will not perish, but have everlasting life.

"That our part of salvation is to trust should not surprise us. Do you remember why Adam was put out of the Garden? It was because he wanted to be independent of God's control. He wanted to trust himself, and his ability to judge what was good for him and what was evil for him—rather than trust God. If we got into trouble because we didn't want to depend on God, what would you think God would require for us to come home? The obvious answer is that we must return the way we left; we must again choose to be dependent on God, rather than self.

---

1. Henry M. Morris, *The Genesis Record* (Grand Rapids: Baker Book House, 1977), p. 41.